# THE *Art* OF ENTERTAINMENT

## A Producer's Sourcebook
## for Choral Performance

by
FRITZ MOUNTFORD

Foreword and Commentary
by
JOHN JACOBSON

Editor's Note: The pictures in this book feature Fritz Mountford's Ball State University Singers in rehearsal, performance and on the road.  Photographs by Ball State University Photo Service

**Hal Leonard Publishing Corporation**
7777 West Bluemound Road  P.O. Box 13819  Milwaukee, WI  53213

This book is gratefully dedicated

to the memory of

**FRED WARING**

American Showman

1900-1984

# CONTENTS

# Contents

# Contents

# Contents

# Contents

# Contents

# FOREWORD
## by
### John Jacobson

A small child saves his pennies for months and then marches down to the local dime-store to purchase the coveted model airplane that has been displayed in the store window since before the holiday rush. He races home and spreads out all of the components on the kitchen table. There are hundreds of pieces. He notes the left and right wings and aerilons. He checks off the flaps, the propeller, the fuselage and even the cockpit with accompanying pilot and ejector seat. He shakes with anticipation as he fingers the decals and admires the brightly colored paints. He's got the glue, the newspapers to spread over the table for protection, the paint brushes and even the case in which to display the final product. He knows that he has what it takes to get the job done. He learned gluing in kindergarten. He mastered paints in first grade and conquered large motor skills in second. He breezed through vocabulary tests in the third grade and by the fourth could read the directions of even a very complicated book of instructions. Instructions? Oh, my goodness, the manufacturing company has somehow left out the forty-four page instructional manual that can lead the young hobbiest through the many steps that it will take to transform all of these disjointed elements into an F-14 Starfighter! What good are all of these parts if the builder doesn't know where to begin or where to end in the construction of the final product? Nobody told him this would happen when he graduated from fourth grade to middle school!!

A young family piled into the spanking new Chevy well before sunrise. They had tied the sturdy suitcases to the rooftop carrier, packed a basket full of snacks and a good solid lunch so they wouldn't have to stop for hours. They buckled up for safety as the three-week, eagerly anticipated tour-of-the-country was about to begin. Both Mother and Father were expert drivers and would share that responsibility. Missy made sure that the pets were cared for. Sonny had emptied his piggy bank of all its contents for extra cash en route and Junior, with his Weekly Reader, had accurately researched the many historical sights that they would witness along the way. Cameras were ready and the first-aid kit was stowed. All elements of a successful vacation seemed in place. Father shifted the car into first gear and smoothly rolled to the end of the driveway. "O.K.," he asked spritely, "Which way do we go?" The words echoed like a time bomb! The entire spirit of the carload sank instantaneously. No one had provided a map!

(O.K. O.K. I'm getting to the point!)

All those feisty music teachers study piano from the age of four and voice

> "What good are all these parts if the builder doesn't know where to begin or where to end in the construction of the final product?"

*from six-and-a-half. They are on their way to being experts when they graduate from high school and then go on for four to ten more years of higher education to fully qualify themselves as educators. They study the history of their art and master its theory and execution. They take classes in the techniques of education so that they may be more effective in their own classrooms and with their own students. They accept a teaching job feeling fully qualified that they can enhance the lives of the people that they are to instruct. They go to their very first choral directors' conference and come away absolutely shell-shocked! "Those people in there are lunatics! They were talking about public relations and fund-raising as if that were a significant part of their jobs! They were talking about press releases, budgeting and costumes as if they spend a load of time dealing with that! What in the world is 'choralography', a 'zero stance' or a 'poof for heaven's sake!? That was the head of my own music department in there talking about reversible skirts and beige character shoes! I'm a teacher, not Cecil B. DeMille!!"*

**"They came away absolutely shell-shocked! I'm a teacher, not Cecil B. DeMille!"**

*How many of you feel at times like you must have missed a class somewhere as an undergraduate in music education? How many have asked, "Why didn't somebody tell me I had to know all of this?" How many of you often wonder, "Did someone forget to include the instruction manual?" or "Where's the map that will tell me how to put all that I know together into a work of art?"*

*Ponder for a moment the state of musical composition if there were no rules and guidelines that governed it. Imagine that composers and arrangers simply ignored the historic precedents of chord structure and voice leading or the terminology that has become standard equipment in the dynamic art of making music. Frightening, isn't it? Yet, up to now, that is precisely what we have been asked to do in regard to the equally dynamic art of making entertainment. By ignoring the subject, our own instructors and institutions have been suggesting that there are no guidelines available; no historical role models or precedents to follow. By not addressing **The Art of Entertainment** we've been led to believe that the very concrete theory of entertainment, unlike the theory of music, does not exist.*

*Still, we find ourselves in positions of leadership where our "expertise", not only in the production of music but also in promotion, publicity, costumes, and choreography is expected. More startling yet is that we look around us and see that our peers are finding themselves in the very same proverbial ship and that, surprisingly enough, it's not sinking! Somehow, by trial and error, hit and miss, or plain dumb luck their programs are surviving. In fact, their programs are flourishing!*

*With a closer look you discover that these successful peers really DO know something that you THOUGHT you didn't!*

They've discovered that there really are rules and guidelines that define good entertainment. They've realized that there ARE historical precedents set by such greats as Walt Disney, Fred Waring, Al Jolson, Duke Ellington, Leonard Bernstein, Gilbert and Sullivan, George and Ira Gershwin, Charlie Chaplin; YES! Ziegfield, DeMille, Astaire and even Wolfgang Amadeus Mozart!! Successful educators appreciate that these precedents constitute the absolutely legitimate theory of **The Art Of Entertainment!**

The trouble is, nobody ever wrote it all down! There's been no map! That is, until now.

Fritz Mountford is a scholar of the theory of entertainment. For years he has studied it, performed it and lived it! His teachers have been some of the greats that made the molds. Now, he shares his research with all of us so that we can all be better at what we do. We don't have to be afraid of something that we never understood. Now we have a manual of instruction, a map for our art. Certainly, like any art form, ours will continue to grow and change. But, the growth will be progress instead of floundering. **The Art of Entertainment** is legitimate! Here are the things they never taught you at the Conservatory Music School! (With a few theories of my own thrown in for good measure.) Enjoy!

John Jacobson
Washington D. C.
Winter 1990

*"There really are rules and guidelines that define good entertainment. Now we have a manual of instruction, a map for our art."*

Editor's Note: John's observations and comments appear in italics throughout this book.

# PREFACE

Whenever I speak at a convention or in-service day, whenever I rehearse a festival choir or conduct an honors chorus, whenever I teach at a summer camp or workshop, I am always asked one question: "Where do you get all your energy?" My answer is usually something like, "We've got a lot to do in a short amount of time," or "I just feel a great passion for what we're doing." My *real* answer is "You know, I really don't have any energy at all; I just share what others have shared with me!" It takes some explaining:

I'm one of those people who believe that energy isn't something you can *get*. Energy isn't something you can *have*. Energy bounces around everywhere, all the time; all you have to do is plug in! Energy rushes out through me to you because so much energy rushes into me through so many other people. All the professional entertainers and educators I know have become part of an energy-filled network I call **The Art of Entertainment**. I've been lucky to learn a lot from them. This book is my attempt to start to share their creative energy with you.

I've always been a question-asker, a note-taker and an outline-maker. I like to get things organized. One summer, I was trying to file the notes I'd taken at a choral workshop in Washington. I decided that several bits and pieces didn't fit any of the categories I had established in college, so I dropped them in an empty file folder and labeled it "SEATTLE." Since then, my "Seattle File" has outgrown the file folder and is threatening to overflow a four-drawer file cabinet! **The Art of Entertainment** will never quite fit any of the categories you learned in college, but you'll find invaluable energy in these bits and pieces.

*"The Art of Entertainment will never quite fit any of the categories you learned in college."*

Somewhere along the way, other people started asking me questions (as though I knew any answers!). They seemed to feel that I had something to share, so I started giving answers based on my observations and experience. I've been lucky to have had some wonderful experiences.

I was first put in the position of "choral clinician" at the Fred Waring Music Workshop. Imagine yourself as a first-year teacher from Red Cloud, Nebraska, standing on the podium in front of two hundred seasoned music educators. They have come from all over the world to study the philosophy and techniques of professional choral entertainment from the man who pretty nearly invented the whole idea in the first place. What will you say? What will you do?

Now, picture Fred Waring himself sitting just behind your left shoulder during the entire rehearsal! He's not just watching. He's not just listening. He's talking quietly in your ear: "That's it? You're satisfied with that sound? Where's the melody? Don't let them hiss and spit. You think an audience will understand those words? Don't sing Voice...sing Songs." I learned a lot in a hurry!

*"Your activities revolve around planning, preparing and presenting The Show."*

Later, I had a chance to work as a vocal coach at Disneyland and at Walt Disney World. I was thrilled to discover that the things I had learned from Fred Waring were true all over the entertainment industry. I believe in the Disney concept of *The Show:* Every facet of the work done by your "entertainment organization" is part of the same, wide picture. Some of the work is done Backstage, out of view of the audience, and some of the work— the part you usually think of as "show"— is done Onstage. Your activities revolve around planning, preparing, and presenting *The Show.*

A printed version of my Art of Entertainment/Seattle File first appeared when my lecture notes for a series of presentations to the European Council of Independent Schools were condensed in an issue of the Choral Journal of the American Choral Directors Association. The information was expanded to become the core of a "Participant's Handbook" for the Brightleaf Music Workshop.

This book is still just a collection of bits and pieces. Sometimes they are in alphabetical order; more often they aren't. Sometimes I'm writing to you as an experienced teacher, or as a student, or as an aspiring entertainer— but always in the spirit of sharing. It is meant to be the start of your own Seattle File. I hope you'll discover it while you are still in college, so you'll have a chance to fill the margins with your own notes, arguments and ideas. I hope it will become one of the dog-eared, coffee-stained resources that never has a chance to gather dust on your reference shelf. I hope it will become one of the "browsing" books you take to the cabin every August as you begin to focus your energy for the coming school year.

I can't begin to acknowledge by name all the people who are part of my personal system of energy and information. You'll just have to take my word that they are all very good at what they do. My parents and family first encouraged my uninhibited self-expression. The neighbors allowed backyard circuses and make-believe operas, piano lessons, a drum set, a very loud five-string banjo, Indian dancers, and the Ponderer. They shook their heads in disbelief sometimes, but they let me *try*.  I sure hope the people in *your* hometown still support opportunities for kids to explore the whole range of artistic, intellectual, physical, and emotional experience.  (I also hope that *you* pause every-so-often to remember that little kid who still lives inside your head and heart; the kid who first fell in love with whatever passion it is that makes you tick!)

My college friends and teachers encouraged me to specialize in singing and introduced me to the self-discipline of the practice room and commitment to regular rehearsals.  They endured my trials and errors as I began to experiment with directing and conducting.  It was their open-minded support that led to the start of my professional career, playing the honky-tonk piano in an Old West saloon!  I'm very proud of that fact, and hope that you'll be inspired to go out and encourage one of your own students to risk a "peculiar" career!

I find remarkable energy through every person I meet everywhere around the country.  Thanks, as always, to my professional associates, colleagues, students, and friends.  They sometimes shake their heads in disbelief, too!  To countless singers, dancers, instrumentalists, and technicians who willingly allow me to continue to experiment, and to their teachers, administrators, and audiences who contribute to (or stay out of the way of) the flow of energy, thank you!

In dedicating this book to the memory of Mr. Waring, I intend to express my gratitude to everyone who was involved in his dynamic and creative entertainment organization.  It is a sad fact that, in professional show business, some people think they are in the spotlight because they *hold* a certain amount of energy and knowledge.  To the contrary, the remarkable people Mr. Waring gathered around himself spent their lives *sharing* experience and knowledge and caring in every direction. From Ray Sax Schroeder and from Rich Taylor, who each had the ability to condense and to refine the energy and information that flowed through them, I learned to cherish the details of *The Show* that surrounds the beautiful music.  Thank you.

I want to personalize just three other "energizers" from my network of knowledge and energy.  Brian Breed, Stevie Rivers Rawlings, and John Jacobson will recognize that they discovered and articulated many of the concepts in this book long before they shared the ideas with me. I've spent so long being inspired and challenged and supported by each of them that I honestly don't recall who said what when!  That's

*"I learned to cherish the details of **The Show** that surround the beautiful music."*

# Preface

the way a system of energy works.  We all believe that we have an obligation to share what we've been lucky enough to learn. Please turn the page and become part of the network, part of the system. Welcome. Thanks for sharing!


Fritz Mountford
Ball State University
Muncie, Indiana
Winter 1990

*John Jacobson guides readers and viewers through Fritz Mountford's innovative approach to choral performance in The Art Of Entertainment Sourcebook and companion video.*

# Introduction:  The Show

"Why are you putting on a show?"

This is a basic question.  It is a question that is seldom asked and even less frequently answered.

Don't confuse it with the often-asked question, "Why is a show being put on?"  Those answers come easily to mind:  "to challenge my students," "to raise money," "to attract an audience," "to recruit new members," "to please the administration."  The answers are right, but, for the moment, the question is wrong.

Look at my question this way:  "Why are YOU putting on a show?"

YOUR answer to this basic question will affect your approach to the contents of this book.  Here are a million ideas on WHERE and WHEN and HOW to spend an enormous amount of time, energy, and money — yours and everyone else's.  I've designed this book to answer the questions, "WHAT DO I DO?" and "HOW DO I DO IT?".  First, though, I want *you* to be able to answer "WHY AM I DOING WHAT I AM DOING?".

After you know WHY, it will make more sense to ask WHAT and HOW.

Here are three different answers.  It doesn't really matter which of them feels right for YOU.  It does matter that you know which of them is your answer for now.

1) "Entertainment is fun."  Good answer!  As you scan this book, ignore the long-winded philosophy and most of the details.  Just put together some music, some talent, some ideas, and present the result to an audience.  ("My dad's got a barn...!")  Do it just for the pleasure that entertainment brings to people on both sides of the footlights.  You'll go back to your everyday routine with the memory of a terrific experience.  That's a plenty good reason.

2) "Entertainment is interesting."  Perhaps you've reached a certain level of experience and achievement.  Now, you're interested in increasing your bag of tricks; taking a structured approach to the actual experience of producing a show.  Instead of just throwing things together, you should be sitting down and planning each production, thinking about your ideas and how to realize them.  I hope this book will be a guide as you learn to focus your projects: planning, preparing, and presenting *The Show*.  Each time you ring down the curtain on another production you'll feel double satisfaction — both from the show itself, and from knowing how you put it together!

*"Each time you ring down the curtain on another production, you'll feel double satisfaction."*

3) "Entertainment is everything." At this level of involvement, entertainment is more than a diversion, more than a process. For you, *The Show* is an expression of your Self. If you really want to be a producer, then **The Art of Entertainment** becomes part of everything you do. Every day, no matter what you're involved in, your mind will be occupied with the "show-biz" aspects of the activity. If you dream of a life-long career in any facet of entertainment you must know that it is a *serious* commitment. "Putting on a show" becomes much more than enjoyable or rewarding. In fact, the more you achieve, the more you demand of yourself and others, the less you may enjoy the process and the final results! The reward is in the effort, not the achievement. For you this book is just a glimpse at the passion I feel for what I do.

> *"The reward is in the effort, not the achievement."*

Finally: these aren't the only answers and none of them is exclusive. At times, the most casual showman looks for something greater; the most dedicated professional stops to rediscover the fun. *Your* answer will undoubtedly change from time to time. Struggling with the question WHY makes the WHAT and HOW that much more rewarding. Now roll up your sleeves and let's get to work!

This book is divided into three major sections, *Planning The Show*, *Preparing The Show* and *Presenting The Show*. Following John's background observations on each major topic, you'll find a variety of subheadings. Entries under each of these subheadings present the philosophies and techniques that are the heart and soul of **The Art of Entertainment.**

Don't expect a step-by-step, paint-by-number approach to creating *The Show*. You won't find specific repertoire neatly routined and choreographed ready for you to teach your choir. This isn't a pre-assembled, pre-painted, free-home-delivery Furniture Store. Rather, it is a Hardware Store; here are nuts and bolts and nails and planks and hinges organized in a general sort of order. Use them in combination with the tools you've developed as a music educator to build your own unique something-or-other.

Ready? Curtain going up. On with the show!

THE *Art* OF
ENTERTAINMENT™

# I

# PLANNING
# THE SHOW

*"Ultimate Glitz"*

1. **Teacher as Producer**

2. **Creativity**

3. **Terminology**

4. **Auditions**

5. **Repertoire**

6. **Costumes**

7. **Publicity**

8. **Public Relations**

# "Ultimate Glitz"

I'll never forget the day that Gary Paben, Manager of Special Events at Walt Disney World, bounded into the office we shared above Mainstreet U.S.A., literally leapt on top of his desk, spread his arms and cried, "Hey John! We got the GOODYEAR™ Blimp!" What followed has to have been the most profound example of "Glitz" that I, or anyone else, have ever witnessed! Anyone who knows Gary would certainly not be surprised at his less-than-subtle display of enthusiasm. But in this particular instance the news was such a topper that it wasn't long before I was up on the desk with him, dancing on our scripts, jumping up and down on artist's renderings and screeching out a rowdy rendition of "Who's The Leader Of The Club...!"

The thing that really would surprise a stranger to our Entertainment Division offices was that none of the other people in the office area even blinked an eye or came running to see if we had finally flipped. I guess the Halloween show we did the week before with a tap dancing Frankenstein and a forty-foot tall, singing Dracula had already convinced them of our insanity. A simple soft shoe on a roll top was relatively run-o'-the-mill!

Nonetheless, "getting the GOODYEAR™ Blimp" was worthy of excitement for the two of us; excitement that didn't wane until the dirigible had done its thing and the cleat-marked desk was replaced with a runway!

The hoopla centered around the fact that Gary and I were in charge of putting together a production that would appropriately serve as the grand opening celebration of the new airport in Orlando, Florida. Actually, the board of directors for the airport had approached us to produce what they labeled as "an entertaining ribbon cutting ceremony with a few dignitaries, a few speeches and a low budget."

The budget was only a few thousand dollars. That might seem like a fortune to most music educators who realize that that figure probably represents their entire music program's allotment during their thirty-five year career as a teacher. But, when you start having to pay union rates for all of your performers, technical people, rehearsal time, props, etc., it really doesn't amount to much at all. What it does do is force creative thinking to its limits, not to mention creative budgeting!

A few weeks later we had what I would label "a million dollar pile of glitz" and entertainment at its biggest, if not its best.

The entire ceremony, which took place in and above the new airport's giant parking lots, lasted less than twenty minutes. Those twenty minutes included participation by the U.S. Marine Corps Band, sky

> *"A tap dancing Frankenstein and a forty-foot tall, singing Dracula had already convinced them of our insanity."*

*divers holding American flags as they descended, a dozen Rolls Royces delivering the dignitaries, eight rolling staircases used to unload planes, now filled with representative flight attendants from their respective airline companies, forty dancers on six decorated hydraulic lifts normally used in putting food into airplanes, fifty choreographed signal flag personnel on the roof of the airport, two-hundred American flags and bearers on another level of the airport façade, eighty volunteer dancers and thirty-six professional dancers, a full orchestra, thirty-six students carrying sixteen-foot banners bigger than themselves, fourteen choreographed bi-planes, two stunt pilots and their planes making patterns with smoke in the sky, literally tons of fireworks, twenty-thousand helium balloons, eighteen Air Force jets with colored smoke trails, hundreds of white doves, a DC-10, a 747 and, oh yes, the GOODYEAR™ Blimp! The only thing I can think of that we forgot was a ribbon cutting!*

*It was the kind of production that can never be fully rehearsed. You wind up practicing each segment on its own and hope that what is happening in your mind is also going to happen during that one shot performance. Luckily, except for the fact that we nearly burned down the brand new airport with an overdose of fireworks and the reality that the airport's maintenance personnel were still calling us weeks later begging us to come back and collect our pigeons (we called them doves!), who were messing up their skylights, it was a "flying" success! Best of all, it made me even more aware of the inexhaustible possibilities in entertainment and the reality that a little "glitz" (or a lot) can make even a simple "ribbon cutting" into a memorable experience.*

*The real moral of this "ultimate glitz" story is one that might serve as an introduction to the first chapter of **The Art of Entertainment**, that is, the Planning.*

*Long before Gary Paben had made his flying leap onto my homework we knew that our production, of whatever scale, was going to be a soaring success. The reason for our confidence did not have anything to do with aircraft, fireworks or even pigeons. The one element of quality we knew we had secure was the foundation of our entire production. That foundation was the music. Long before any choreography was taught, costumes designed or balloons inflated, the music had been chosen and rehearsed. We knew, through our ears and our hearts, that if all we did was play the music the event would still be moving and memorable. It would be a musical work of art. Hence, the great joy for us as producers was the fact that anything that we added to that already successful foundation would simply amplify it and embellish its effectiveness. Every banner, flag, balloon or blimp would be the frosting on an already tasty dessert. All it took was an incredible, yet feasible, amount of planning.*

**"One element was the foundation of our production. That foundation was the music."**

This chapter is about the planning that needs to go into your own entertainment projects. Large or small the requirements are the same. You, too, will realize that the music is the core, but, that there are many more elements that will top your cake. Your costumes, publicity and promotion are similar to our flight plan and trial runs. You, too, can dream a dream, begin with the music, add any number of accessory elements and see that dream become a reality. What it takes is a calculated and informed plan of action. A plan of action that producers of professional entertainment have used for ages.

Of course, I'm not about to suggest that all of you should attempt to have fourteen bi-planes, the Marine Band and Air Force jets in your next rendition of "Fly Me To The Moon..." After all, most high school or college auditoriums are not nearly that large! But, perhaps the suggestions in the ensuing pages will help you deal with some of those problems that you come up against every year and will aid you in developing your own approach to music-plus. Then, if you want to add the GOODYEAR™ Blimp to your next spring concert you'll have Gary and I to back you up and these pages as a humble written authority that it can be done!

# 1. TEACHER AS PRODUCER

## COMMON JOB DESCRIPTION

The time of year for "District Contest" rolls around. You shift into overdrive in order to: choose new music for soloists and ensembles, order extra copies for the judges, rehearse the music, assign students to number measures in the scores, schedule after-school rehearsals with the accompanists, send home travel notices to be signed and returned, re-number the judges scores correctly, send in a complete application and time-request for each soloist and ensemble, rehearse the music, total the entrance fees, take a check-request form to the central office, request a bus-request form from the transportation office, make phone calls to solve conflicts in assigned performance times, collect lunch money, post the dress and conduct code, rehearse the music, send home second-requests for permission slips, rehearse the music, arrange to borrow three extra robes from the Methodist church, call back to borrow five extra folders, cancel your dentist appointment...

Whew! Does this sound familiar? "Rush Around!" "Put Out Fires!" "The more I do, the more I have to do!"

PERFORMERS are put in charge of moment-to-moment *activity* — "what do I *do* next?"

DIRECTORS are in charge of day-to-day *problem-solving* — "how do we get things done?"

PRODUCERS take charge of long-range *creativity* — "what things *should* we be doing?"

As effective Music Educators, we are Performers all of the time and Directors most of the time. Take time to be a Producer some of the time!

## TEACHER-AS-DIRECTOR

Given a moment to step back and catch your breath, you'll recognize the flaw in this "District Contest" project: lack of delegation. Give yourself a *new* job description: Teacher-as-Director. As the Director your role is to:

1. Let everyone know what the *current project* is.
2. *Explain* the things that need to be done.
3. Establish a *schedule.*
4. *Assign* everyone a responsibility.
5. Keep track of everyone's *progress.*

> *"Step back and catch your breath. Give yourself a new job description."*

6. Let everyone know the *current state of affairs.*
7. *Remind* them of 1-6.

That's better. Now you are in the relative calm of the *eye* of the whirlwind rather than caught in the rush itself. You'll eventually get to District Contest and will have accomplished all the details without having to cancel your visit to the dentist!

## TEACHER-AS-PRODUCER

In your role as organization leader, you'll need to go one step further. Give yourself a job description called Teacher-as-Producer:

1. Decide whether or not we *should* be doing whatever we are doing.
2. Create a vivid "vision" of the *importance* of what we *ought* to be doing.
3. *Focus* everyone's attention on the important vision.
4. Enlist *commitment* to the project— explain *why*, not just *how*.
5. Instill *confidence* in everyone's ability to *share* in the process.

Stop. Breathe. Relax. Reflect. Should we be going to contest at all? Does it support our overall goals and purpose? Is the "return" worth the "investment" of time, energy, and money? What else might we do with the same time, energy, and money? What does so-and-so do? Why? Where did they get that idea, anyway?

*"The important thing is to stop long enough to look at the long view."*

Each Producer will have different answers to these questions. Each Leader will probably ask different questions. The answers aren't really important; the questions aren't even important. The important thing is to *stop* long enough to look at the long view. *Stop* putting out fires. I don't suggest you suddenly flop down in the middle of the choir room on Wednesday morning, but do force yourself to set aside an evening or a weekend or a week. (Don't confuse this special time with the time you ordinarily set aside to choose next year's music or draw up your proposed concert schedule.) Ask big questions. Consider big answers.

Once you've seen the Big Picture, tell it to everyone around you. Tell them early and often. *Sell* it to everyone around you. Once *they've* seen the Big Picture, it doesn't make sense to quibble over the details; everyone wants on a Band Wagon that is headed in an *evident* direction!

When you stop to think about it, your role as Producer is just like your role as ensemble Conductor! The actual music is produced only by members of the choir. As Conductor, you are responsible for seeing that each person sings the right notes at the right time. You establish tempo, volume, and character so that everyone's contribution blends into an artistic whole. You inspire each performer to do his best. No one expects you to sing every note yourself. That's not the Conductor's job!

In your organization, no one expects you to do every job yourself. That's not the Producer's job! The actual work is done by others. As Producer, you are responsible for seeing that the right people do the right things at the right time. You establish the proper schedule, pace, and desired outcome so that individual jobs contribute to the whole project. You inspire each person to do his best.

Don't rush around. Don't put out fires. It's not your job!

## ENTERTAINMENT VALUE

Next Monday morning, as you are brushing your teeth, look in the mirror and *see* a Producer! "I am a Producer." You'll feel foolish at first, knowing that you are on your way to rehearse sixty Eighth-graders in the bus barn in a town that is smaller than (fill in the blank), in a state that is more isolated than (fill in the blank), for an administration that is (blankety-blank!).

Try it again on Tuesday morning. "I am a Producer." Re-read the section of this book called TERMINOLOGY.(See p.13) Review your own list of show business terms that describe what you do.

Wednesday morning: "I am a Producer." Realize that, on Monday morning, somebody somewhere used *your* town or *your* state to fill in the blanks. You've got a lot more than they think they've got!

Thursday morning: "I am a Producer." Consider the dollars-and-cents *value* of what you do. Consider exactly what you are in charge of. Consider just the first two minutes of your up-coming show:

> The opening number will last one-minute-and-twenty-seconds. You'll be well into the next number within the first two minutes. Let's figure out the *value* of mounting just two minutes of entertainment.

> What is the cost of sixty copies of music for the first song and sixty copies of the second song? Plus a few extras for you and the pianist and the drummer? Average $1.00 per copy? Plus postage? **Value of music:  $130**

> It takes about an hour to introduce one minute's worth of choreography. It takes about the same amount of time to learn the same

*"Next Monday morning, as you are brushing your teeth, look in the mirror and see a Producer!"*

amount of music. Your kids will spend more than 240 man-hours (2 hours choreography rehearsal plus 2 hours vocal rehearsal times 60 performers) preparing and polishing the music. This represents what value if you were to pay them minimum wage? But wait! Your kids are skilled performers. They have spent years learning to sing and dance. Pay them each $10 an hour.
**Value of performer's rehearsal time: $2,400**

Costumes. Your kids can't perform naked. What does it cost to clothe a kid? Go out and price a nice dress, and shoes, and accessories, and a suit, and shirt, and tie, and belt, and under-wear... Even if you don't invest in fancy costumes, but have each student wear his or her "Sunday best", what is the value, *per student*, of the clothes on their backs? $90? $125? More? Figure $100 each.
**Value of costumes: $6,000**

What is the value of *your* rehearsal time? (Not what you are actually paid, but the *value*!) Well, what is the value of your professional doctor's time? Take a moment to honestly recall your years of training and experience. Pay yourself $100 an hour. Now, how much time did you spend choosing the music?
**Value of Producer/Director's time: $500**

What is the value of your accompanist's time and training? Those $2 lessons every week since third grade do add up!
**Value of accompanist's time: $250**

Your accompanist will need a piano for rehearsals and perform-ance. (Of course the school *provides* a piano, but you couldn't do your two minutes without it!)
**Value of piano: $3,000**

Will you need to have it tuned?
**Value: $40**

Do you begin to get the picture? How many risers will you need for sixty kids? **Value: $1000.** What is your drum set worth? **$1500.** Do you have an acoustic shell? Curtains on-stage? Theatrical lighting? Chairs for the audience? Heat and lights in the auditorium or gym? Printing of tickets and programs?

Excuse me, but toothpaste is running down your chin. In the first two minutes of your show, you are presenting at least **$10,000** worth of entertainment. And *you* are in charge of every detail. And you do this day after day, year after year.

Friday morning: **"I *am* a Producer!"**

> *"You are presenting at least $10,000 worth of entertainment. Excuse me, but toothpaste is running down your chin!"*

# 2. CREATIVITY

When someone mentions creativity, I'm afraid we picture a quasi-miraculous process in which some totally new idea, full-grown, remarkable, and perfect in every detail, appears out of the void. Creativity in entertainment is not at all mysterious. Creativity is simply a matter of constant borrowing and twisting and trying, then starting again "from the top."

## STEALING IDEAS

Edison said, "To have good ideas, have lots of them" — an idea he got from someone else. Maybe he should have said, "To have good ideas, *steal* lots of them!" We are constantly surrounded by entertainment of every kind. As you develop your "producer's eye," you'll begin to find all sorts of ideas that, approached from a slightly different angle, would work in *your* project. My Seattle File is the dumping place for all the stolen quotes and steps and interpretations and outlines and color schemes and concepts and photographs and designs and programs that I continue to collect at every opportunity. My only defense is that the genesis of each of the ideas I've "collected" was an idea originally swiped from some other thief!

*"Edison said, 'To have good ideas, have lots of them!' An idea he got from someone else."*

## CREATIVE PEOPLE

Surround yourself with creative people, people who also are always on the lookout for ideas that work. Look for people who stimulate your thinking. Ask them "what if ?" and "so what?" questions. (Sometimes *my* best ideas are responses to the challenge "impossible!" "Oh yeah," I say, "well what if we...?") Don't set yourself up as the absolute authority on a given subject. Don't be afraid to play dumb in order to extract an explanation of something you already know about. Be open for the one bit of new information or new angle hidden amongst the same old stuff.

## INSPIRATION

Once you've got a few ideas (no matter the source), start looking at them from funny angles. It helps to be a little crazy, and to surround yourself with crazy people who won't stomp on your enthusiasm. Don't try to do or think anything *new*; just come up with peculiar ways of using what you've already got. If there is a certain time or place that lets you feel free to dream and wonder and fiddle with ideas, go there. Set aside that time and place for coming up with ridiculous answers to "what if ?" and "so what?"

# Creativity

*"Surround yourself with crazy people who won't stomp on your enthusiasm."*

## CHERISHING

It takes all the confidence you can muster to bring an idea to life. When, at last, a really good idea hits you between the eyes, or just begins to creep into your mind, guard it jealously. A lot of great, creative ideas die because they are revealed too early to the cynics and nay-sayers. Try out your new idea on someone who is likely to accept it. You'll realize if it is really off-base as you struggle to explain it. Once you are confident of your idea, *then* hold it up to the 'yeah-but' people. They will rightly shoot down your most outlandish propositions, but your terrific ideas will have the strength to get through!

## DEADLINES

Finally, impose a deadline for having a solution to a problem. You may end up with a not-quite-right solution, but activity generates thought and in the middle of implementing the near-miss, someone is likely to come up with the just-right solution.

# 3. TERMINOLOGY

Begin to cloak your endeavors in the magic aura of Entertainment. Part of the magic is known to everyone: you can put a yellow dress on stage, then with lights, make it turn red or orange or green or white — magic! Another part of the magic is subliminal, but just as effective: you can put an idea into people's minds, then make it change color, too. Familiar or innovative, intimate or extravagant, ordinary or exciting.

Names and titles really *do* change attitudes and approaches— both your own and those of your students, I mean your "aspiring young entertainers!" Some of these terms are standard theatre jargon (most show-biz terms appear in the book without definition), but they are presented here with a philosophical statement that will start you thinking in a new way (or support the entertainment ideas you already use).

*"Names and titles really do change attitudes and approaches."*

### BACKSTAGE
In a narrow definition, BACKSTAGE is the area of the theatre not seen by the audience. Expand your definition to include all your rehearsal sites, costume and scenery construction, program preparation and printing. Suddenly, your whole school becomes BACKSTAGE! Also consider the work done BACKSTAGE before, during, and after your show, to be a valuable and integral part of the entire production. It is easy to fall into the deadly trap of thinking of Onstage performers as the "stars" while BACKSTAGE contributors are only "techies" or "gofers." The success of your show relies equally on visible and "invisible" contributions!

### BOX OFFICE
The name given to the place at the theatre where tickets are sold. You may have a little glassed-in booth, or a card table and cigar box, or somebody's home phone number — call them all BOX OFFICE. Satellite places — the drug store, insurance agency, or supermarket — are called TICKET OUTLETS. Use them, too.

### COSTUMES/OUTFITS
Entertainers wear *costumes* to perform; girlfriends wear *outfits* to the movies. If your costume has been tailor-made especially for you or just brought-from-home, you move and act in a special way when you are dressed in something called a COSTUME.

### DIRECTOR
The title you give yourself affects the way everyone — performers, audience, administration— thinks of you. Some mysterious eleva-

*"Reach out over the footlights to include your audience, your guests, in the entertainment you have planned for their enjoyment."*

tion in status occurs when you redefine your role from "school teacher" to PRODUCER/DIRECTOR. They probably won't call you "maestro", but they might start to think of you that way!

## ENTERTAINERS/PERFORMERS

Performers simply sing their songs in a room; ENTERTAINERS *fill* the room with their songs. Performers expect an audience to sit back and intellectually observe, while ENTERTAINERS encourage the audience to get emotionally and physically involved. Reach out over the foot-lights to *include* your audience, your guests, in the entertainment you have planned for their enjoyment. I tend to use PERFORMERS and ENTERTAINERS interchangeably, but I'm thinking "audience-oriented" in both cases.

## FUND RAISING

The name FUND RAISING seems to have more class than "Money Making Project." "Our goal isn't the *money*. It is, rather, the Event or Activity made possible by the contribution that demonstrates your loyal support."

## HOUSE

The part of your theatre where the audience sits. Your HOUSE may be just the north end of the cafeteria, but change its name and it becomes part of *The Show*!

## ONSTAGE

The same philosophy as BACKSTAGE. Don't encourage your ONSTAGE personnel to become Prima Donnas. Also, let every cast member be aware that *The Show* begins as soon as he or she is visible ONSTAGE. There is no Kings-X or Time Out while you wander onstage, find the music, tune the flute, adjust the piano stool... it's just like fishing: as soon as you see the fish, they see you. If you're on tour or performing at the Mall or for the Rotary luncheon, ONSTAGE expands to mean every place and situation you are seen as representing your organization. Every time you step off the bus and into a restaurant, the curtain goes up and you're ONSTAGE. An important burden.

## PRODUCER

The person who pulls all the strings and has final authority and responsibility is the Producer. Don't *do* everything yourself, but be sure that it *is* getting done. The cause of Producer's Headache #1 is: the inability to delegate. There is also a Headache #2: realize when you are *not* the producer, when control is out of your hands. Don't agonize over the things you can't fix: someone else's schedule, the weather, a suddenly-out-of-tune piano.

### REHEARSAL/PRACTICE

Football teams practice; actors and musicians REHEARSE. Establish a certain seriousness of purpose and expectation of progress and ultimate achievement for every rehearsal. (To break out of the "school teacher" mode, convince yourself that you are paying every rehearsal participant $114.00 an hour!) *Serious* doesn't need to mean boring or regimented or frightening, but work to build the attitude that excellence is fun; fooling around is just passing time.

### SEASON

Build expectations, involvement, and commitment in your students, administration, and audience toward a year-long *series* of events, not a dissociated string of just-one-more-item-on-our-already-too-full-calendar.

### SET/RISERS, SHOW/CONCERT, THEATRE/AUDITORIUM

The list goes on and on. By this time you get the idea that the names you give things and people and events affect the way they are treated and considered. Throughout this book you'll find that the difference between your college Secondary Methods approach and the Art of Entertainment approach is mostly a matter of detail and point-of-view.

*"The Art of Entertainment approach is mostly a matter of detail and point-of-view."*

Now then, about that "get-together" with your band director and assistant principal— go ahead, schedule your first PRODUCTION MEETING!!

# 4. AUDITIONS

*Talent* and *Chance* must come in the correct percentages to equal a success. You can't control Chance, but you can control your ability to present your Talent. Look at every audition as a learning experience. You are *successful* every time you do your best, or discover how to improve next time — whether or not you get the job. Audition often. Don't wait for your One Big Chance, then "blow it" because of lack of experience.

## TYPE

Often auditioners are looking for a predetermined physical or vocal type. No matter how talented you are, if you aren't a "red-headed-alto-between-5'2"-and-5'4"" you won't be cast. It may not be fair, but it is true.

## TRIPLE-THREAT

Sing, Dance, and Act: Train yourself to be a multi-talented entertainer. Of course everyone will have one area of emphasis, but your chances of getting a part increase if you have had any amount of training and experience in other areas.

## OPPORTUNITY KNOCKS

Start planning and preparing your audition *now* so you'll be ready on a moment's notice. It is a big mistake to wait until the week before an audition to start looking for a perfect song. Spend time *now* trying out material and polishing your act. Then, when the perfect opportunity arises, you won't need to spend time and energy worrying about the basics; you'll be able to concentrate on doing your best!

## TAPED AUDITIONS

Sometimes the door to an in-person audition is opened through a recorded (audio, video, or both) audition. Think of it as an audition "package," not just a cassette tape in a padded mailer.

1. Cassette or reel-to-reel is standard. (Don't send an 8-track tape or a disk. Sure, the auditioners might have access to a playback machine, but it might be a bother to set it up, so your audition could go unheard.)

2. Check the recording level and balance. Make a few 16-bar trials before you go for a "take."

3. As always, select material that fits the job and best showcases your talent. It is always true that first impressions are lasting.

4. Sing your best first, then include a variety to demonstrate your versatility. You can include more on a recording than you would be allowed to sing in a live audition, but the entire tape probably won't be heard. Shorten selections to highlight your strengths.

5. Review your recording! Wait a day or two, then go back and listen with a critical ear. The tape should reflect your talent, personality, and confidence. Re-record any selections that aren't "just right" — a luxury you never get in a live audition!

6. Your audition "package" should include: cover letter, résumé or job application, recent photographs (face and full length), audio tape, and letters of recommendation. (A video tape is great to show dance ability and personality, but is *not* a replacement for a good quality audio tape.)

7. Label (name and address) every component of your "package." It often happens that applications, photos, tapes, and support materials get separated during the review process. Imagine the frustration of wanting to hire "that voice!" but not knowing who is on the tape because the label was only on the little plastic box!

8. Send everything in an appropriate mailer in plenty of time to meet the stated audition deadline. Just as you wouldn't rush into a live audition at the last minute gasping for breath, you should avoid frantic, last-minute phone calls and special delivery mail.

*"First impressions are lasting. Sing your best first, then include a variety to demonstrate your versatility."*

## PURPOSE AND GOAL

The purpose of any interview or audition is simply to get "their" attention. Next, present, in a short span of time, an indication of the *spectrum* of your talent and personality. Some auditions are relaxed and easy-going, others are high-pressure and abrupt.

## LIVE AUDITION

Rehearse the *entire* audition: how to sit, when to stand, even answer imaginary questions. Rehearse under pressure. Rehearse until the entire procedure becomes second nature. *Imagine success!*

1. Be prepared. This is the most important rule; everything else is secondary. Memorize all audition material. Bring your own music

in the correct keys. Arrive early to get familiar with facilities and procedures. Have a variety of material ready. Bring dance clothes and shoes. Bring a snack. Have available a recent photo, résumé, and demo tape—just in case you're asked. (Now you know *why* professionals lug around those ridiculous huge dance bags!)

2. First impressions count. You must look and act as though this audition is an important event. Dress appropriately and comfortably. Pay attention to grooming. Your audition begins the moment you arrive and doesn't end until you are on your way home.

3. Select material that fits the job: Chances are a theme park has limited use for a singer of opera arias; a church choir isn't interested in Top 40 hits. Select material that best showcases your talent: If you're a soprano, sing high notes; basses, sing low notes.

4. Sing your best first. Auditioners *may* only want to hear 8 bars. It would be a shame for them to cut you off while you were just warming up, saving your best for last. Have a contrasting style ready if they want to hear more. Sing *to* the auditioners, but don't feel you have to stare them down. (Chances are, the most influential people sit in the middle.)

5. Shorten selections to highlight your strengths. Skip the piano introduction; skip the verse; go straight for the show-off chorus. Remember, they're not auditioning your *song*, they're auditioning your *voice*. This isn't the time to "introduce" your original composition.

6. Briefly and clearly explain your interpretation to the accompanist. Take care to mark your score beforehand. The accompanist can "make or break" your audition. Be polite. If the pianist fouls up, keep right on singing. They're not auditioning the *piano player*, they're auditioning *you*. As a matter of fact they probably want to hire someone (you!) who has the presence to hang on in the face of disaster. Don't accompany yourself — unless you are absolutely positive that you can give undivided attention and concentration to *both* singing and playing.

> *"Imagine success. Be happy for the opportunity to share your talent."*

7. Be yourself. Know your personality type: if you are "tall, dark, and elegant," don't try to force yourself into the mold "short, blonde, and zany." Focus your concentration on the job at hand: be calm, confident, and alert. Project a positive attitude: be happy for the opportunity to share your talent. Let the answer to every question be, "Yes I Can" or "Yes I'll Try!"

## AUDITIONER

As you begin to put your ideas together, you'll want to know what kind of talent is available to realize your vision. If you are already familiar with your "talent pool" the audition process will likely be impromptu and informal. Be sure, though, to give everyone a chance to "show their stuff." "If you don't try the glass slipper on every foot, you might miss one of your real Cinderellas!"

It may be that you aren't familiar with all the available talent, or you just want to give your students the experience of preparing and presenting a "formal" audition. A talent audition is, after all, great training for all of life's auditions and interviews.

The information and advice presented here has been developed through lots of conversations with teachers and students who aspire to various levels of participation in entertainment. The stereotype of a Broadway "cattle call" (six hours outside in the cold, "take a number," two minutes to warm up, "just leave your coat on," at least straighten my tie, "NEXT!" deep breath and smile, "hellomyname"— "NEXT!") really does exist. I'm not sure its a good model for auditions in general, but the underlying point-of-view that says "be over-prepared, then keep it short and sweet" is valid.

Be a friendly and courteous auditioner. Face it, every performer does better in a supportive atmosphere. Don't sit back in the dark. Do greet each person and double-check names, numbers, or however you identify them. Ask a couple of questions to put them at ease. Pay attention to voice projection, personality, and "naturalness" on a stage. Graciously guide them through the process: "Go ahead and take a minute to show your music to Sally, our accompanist." "Stand right up here and let us have it; you won't mind if we hear only part of your song." Smile. Listen for the first sounds you hear and be aware of your instant reaction. Be willing to forgive at least one false start: "Oops, that's OK, take a deep breath and give it another try. That's OK, don't worry. Now..."

Evaluate quality, pitch, range, musicality, etc., but also try to divine potential and desire. Growing go-getters are more fun through long rehearsals than a crowd of perfect prima-donnas! Decide on a certain minimum time to spend with each auditioner, then give them every chance to make a success. In the long run, your time is wasted only by those who are obviously ill-prepared and marginally committed. Dismiss them politely but do let them know that your production isn't an excuse for a few minutes of thoughtless preparation.

*"If you don't try the glass slipper on every foot, you might miss one of your real Cinderellas!"*

# Auditions

Let each auditioner know when and how the results will be released. Encourage those who aren't selected to keep growing and training and to try again next time. Put those you do select on a "tentative cast list" and "invite them to the first rehearsal." They need to know that passing the audition is only the first step toward living up to your expectations.

*Résumé photos project your personality to the viewer. Notice a stronger "connection" when the focus is directly into the camera lens. An aggressive or playful body position counteracts the square, static quality of the basic "mug shot."*

# 5. REPERTOIRE

There is music of value in every category you can name. There is also "junk" in every category you can name. Search for quality in original compositions and in arrangements and always strive for quality in your preparation and performance.

*"There is music of value in every category you can name. There is also 'junk' in every category you can name."*

## AUDIENCE DIVERSITY

Based on your "audience-oriented" point-of-view, you have an obligation to program material that will appeal to a broad audience. Don't use this as an excuse to reduce everything to a low common denominator. Every single number in your show doesn't have to appeal to every single member of your audience, but, a lot of people should leave a lot of your performances satisfied that *they* were considered in the planning and programming. Try to include "a little something for everyone!"

Be aware that there is both an *actual* and a *perceived* audience for your program. They include the members of your choirs, your student body, the faculty and administration, parents, the community at large, your friends and peers, your teachers, and all of your profession. They all have varied tastes based on varied interest, experience, and training. They are all worthy of consideration; keep them in perspective. As always, be willing to experiment for innovation and vitality.

## HISTORICAL STYLE PERIODS

The "backbone" of our musical tradition. As music educators we owe it to our students and to our audiences to share gems from the past. We have no obligation to preach, bore, or condescend. Of course, your performance is not a theory or music history lecture, but take time to translate foreign texts and to explain a few high points of style or compositional techniques.

## AVANT GARDE

Avant Garde compositions allow you to approach ideas and emotions in new ways — to "hear with new ears." From an audience perspective, beware of works that are interesting primarily from a theoretical point-of-view, works that *are* better than they *sound*! Program Avant Garde in a "variety" context; be sure to surround an unfamiliar (or peculiar) work with music that is more "comfortable." Because Avant Garde is, by definition, experimental, there are few rules as to what is good and bad. Rely on your own judgement and taste in matters of message, performance forces, and amount of rehearsal spent in return for musical and emotional results.

## SACRED

Musical expressions of faith run the gamut from contemporary to historical and from profound to "wahoo!" For forty years my grandparents sang duets at every funeral in our little Nebraska prairie town, so I find hymns and anthems to have great appeal. (Your programming will, of course, reflect your own idiosyncratic and eclectic taste.) Contemporary Christian music is a major force in the current "commercial" scene, as is Contemporary Gospel. A grand musical setting of a Brotherhood or non-religious Inspirational text stands next to the Patriotic Anthem as an ideal finale for any choral concert. And don't forget both historical and popular Hymns to Music!

## VOCAL JAZZ

To my mind there are two broad categories of vocal jazz. The first includes new-made compositions with clever titles in which voices imitate instrumental improvisation. The second includes "standards" or original songs (with poetic texts) in settings that feature contemporary harmonies and inflections. The *song*, then, becomes the point-of-departure for free vocal improvisation. Most audiences relate best to the second category, and even better to settings of *familiar* standards. Vocal Jazz includes a broad range of material including Nostalgia, Standards, Avant Garde, and even Choral Art Songs. Slow tempo ballads offer an excellent opportunity for emotional interpretation and the use of idiomatic vocal techniques.

## CHRISTMAS CAROLS, ANTHEMS and HYMNS

Consider the tremendous variety that is available in songs dealing with the spiritual aspect of Christmas. Some are charged with deep emotion, while others are downright playful. Historical Masterworks are especially appropriate and expected at Christmastime. The secular side of Christmas offers an ever-growing number of popular hits, many of which are considered "standard."

*"Fred Waring always said, 'Folk songs never was wrote, they was just thunk up and did.'"*

## FOLK SONGS

Folk song settings range from frivolous to profound, but they all have a place because they reflect so directly through time and distance the diverse character of the folks who created them. Fred Waring always said, "Folk songs never was wrote, they was just thunk up and did!"

# Repertoire

Some folk songs are transcribed in the simplest way and others are closer to original compositions based on folk themes. For most purposes, there doesn't need to be a clear distinction between Folk Songs and Early Americana, Hymn Tunes, and Spirituals.

## NOVELTY

Too often we think of a Novelty number as a frivolous "throw-away." Think, instead, of a "lighthearted gem" that will contrast to the rest of your program. To be truly effective, novelty numbers must have the same careful preparation as any work from the "standard" repertoire. Granted, some are unabashed Corn, but without some real hokum in your show, how will the audience know how beautiful everything else is?

## POPULAR STANDARDS

The schmaltz of Tin Pan Alley, the sophistication of the Silver Screen and Great White Way, the jump and jive of the Big Band Age: these songs are our musical heritage from the first half of the twentieth century. Some are wrenchingly naive, but their ebullience is honest, so evocative of the eras they represent. Use such bits-of-sparkle with care; they can wear thin in rehearsal or during repeated performances, but will draw that special murmur or sigh of recognition (and warm applause) every time!

On the other hand, the melodies and messages of the "contemporary classics" (works by Gershwin, Kern, Porter, Arlen, and a dozen others) are timeless. True "Standards" lend themselves to new settings and interpretations — that is the hallmark of a classic. The purpose of education is to preserve and transmit culture to each new generation. Here are the keystones of our unique American style. Mr. Waring said it best: "The old songs are the best songs, because if they weren't good enough when first written, they wouldn't have lasted long enough to become 'old' songs."

> *"The old songs are the best songs because if they weren't good enough when first written, they wouldn't have lasted long enough to become 'old' songs."*

## NOSTALGIA

Who's to say how old something must be to qualify as nostalgia? Popular hits of yesterday and the day before have tremendous power to strike a responsive, nostalgic chord in your audience. The first few notes of the introduction or words of the chorus serve as a vivid, personal, and individual reminder of events and places and people from the near past. Naturally, both the silly and serious sides of pop-song culture thrive in every decade!

# Repertoire

## CHORAL ENTERTAINMENT GENRES

Here's a brief outline to introduce a varied, audience-oriented repertoire.  Add your own ideas and favorites to expand the list:

### A. HISTORICAL
1. Chant
2. Renaissance
3. Baroque
4. Classical
5. Romantic
6. Contemporary
7. Avant Garde
8. Other

### B. SACRED
1. Hymn Settings
2. Spirituals
3. Gospel—Traditional/Contemporary
4. Contemporary Christian
5. Inspirational
6. Bible School Songs
7. Other

### C. SECULAR
1. Broadway Show Tunes
   a. standards
   b. contemporary
   c. little known
2. Country
   a. Western
   b. Bluegrass
   c. Rockabilly
3. Folk Songs
   a. Mountain
   b. Sea
   c. Pioneer
   d. Cowboy
   e. Foreign
4. Vocal Jazz
   a. up-tempo rhythmic
   b. close harmony ballad
   c. accompanied solo or duet
5. Top 40 Hits
   a. Rock
   b. Soul
   c. Rhythm & Blues

6. Patriotic
   a.  standard anthems
   b.  "flag wavers" (Cohan, et al.)
7. Other

**D.  POPULAR HISTORICAL**

  1. War Eras— Revolution, Civil War, WW I, WW II
  2. Minstrel
  3. Gay 90's— "The Sentimental Age"
  4. Roaring 20's
  5. Barbershop— Men/Women
  6. Standards of 30's & 40's
  7. Novelty Nostalgia
  8. Swing Era— Big Bands
  9. 50's Rock 'n Roll
10. 60's Protest/Peace/Folk
11. 70's Disco
12. 80's Current Trends— Rap
13. Other

**E.  FEATURES**

  1. Foreign Language
  2. Songs for Children
  3. Speech Chorus
  4. Novelty
  5. Nostalgia
  6. Seasonal/Holiday/Special Occasion
  7. Avant Garde
  8. Movie/TV Themes & Commercials
  9. Other

# 6. COSTUMES

### ADD-ONS

Costumes are expensive. Start with a dress or skirt-and-blouse and trousers-and-shirt and maybe a vest or jacket, and you've already spent a good deal of money. Don't feel you must have a different costume for every different style of song in your show. Give the audience some credit for creativity and think in terms of gently prodding their imaginations. Start with something simple, easy to move in, easy to care for, then add bits and pieces that complement the color scheme of the basic costume, and suggest the style of each new set of songs. As a matter of fact, everyone doesn't need to make every change; just a few of anything can give the effect of a complete change. Here are some ideas to create a turn-of-the-century look over a basic dress. Make your own list for guys. Then think about Twenties, Country, Fifties, Contemporary, Patriotic.

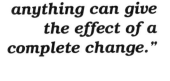

*"Just a few of anything can give the effect of a complete change."*

— long, reversible over-skirt with ruffles
— sheer, long-sleeved over-blouse with Gibson Girl shoulders
— sash or sequined belt with velcro closure
— clip-on tie (bow or long, wide or narrow)
— oversize bow in hair
— wide-brimmed hat with feathers
— straw skimmer

— feathered boa (expensive—one is plenty!)
— frilly apron, long or short
— vest, reversible, velcro closure
— arm garters
— leg garters
— a tie-on bustle and train
— white gloves, long or short
— spats, white or colors
— jacket
— scarf

## BLOCKS OF COLOR

In thinking about costumes, picture not just one individual, but a row or group. How will they look on stage in a cluster? Of course you'll see *blocks* of same-colored skirts and trousers with contrasting blocks of shirts and blouses. Let your mind's eye experiment with blocks that contrast front-and-back or left-and-right as well. Patterns need to be bold to "read" from a distance. Bright, solid colors make each individual seem to be bigger, more important, on stage. A small pattern, even though it may look like a solid from the audience can add the illusion of depth and texture to certain non-reflective fabrics. Avoid little details that may look great close-up but muddy the look from a distance.

*"Avoid little details that may look great close-up but muddy the look from a distance."*

## CLOTHES AS COSTUMES

Even without fancy, matching, made-to-order costumes you can create visual ensemble through attention to color, texture, and line. A group dressed in a long-sleeved, short-sleeved, bow-tie, no-tie, four-in-hand tie, dark-trousers, light-trousers, skirt-and-blouse, party-dress, prom-dress, slacks, vertical-stripe, pastel-pattern, primary-solid won't *sound* like much of an ensemble either! Black skirt & trousers, white blouse & shirt addresses the problem but looks (and sounds), well, boring!

Certain general guidelines can lend an ensemble look. For example:

GIRLS— *knee-length* dress or skirt-and-blouse combination (no dropwaist or Empire 'baby-doll' waist), *solid pastel* or *light colors* (tiny pattern is OK), no opaque or textured stockings, no personal jewelry.

BOYS— *long-sleeves, solid pastel* or *light-colored* shirt with a darker *four-in-hand tie, dark trousers,* and *dark shoes and socks.*

# Costumes

With a little pre-planning and borrowing (have a "costume parade" a few days before your show to leave time for minor changes) your group will *feel* as though they are dressed, in costume, to *perform*.

### CONDUCTOR

The conductor is not a co-equal member of the ensemble. Your costume should be different from the costume worn by the group. It can complement through style, color, texture, and line, but psychologically the conductor should be set apart from the performers. (The exception is, of course, everyone in white tie and tails... you can't dress "up" any more than that. You shouldn't— leave capes, canes, and furs to nineteenth century opera stars!)

On the other hand, the conductor shouldn't be over-dressed in comparison to the ensemble: your austere black formal gown is inappropriate when the singers are in shirt sleeves and everyday skirts and blouses. The age of the singers, time of day, and formality of the occasion make a difference too. HE: an elementary conductor may look *too* imposing in a dark vested suit. SHE: a correct corporate suit and blouse might not be dressy *enough* for an evening of classical music.

Remember, the audience sees mostly your back.

SHE: Avoid a sleeveless gown, sheer back, and any detail on the back of a dress that would draw the eye down to the waist or hem-line. In fact, you might want to wear something (tasteful) in your hair to draw the eye up. Avoid excess jewelry; remember the high-fashion model is frozen, but we see (and hear) you in motion. Beware *high* heels: "A house built on shifting sand can't wave its arms with much authority."

HE: Avoid the bulge of a wallet in your back pocket and creases behind the knees and in the small of your back. Shoes lighter than your trousers draw the eye down— you appear shorter, less in command. Do shine your shoes, do keep your hair off your face. (See GROOMING p.107.)

*"The conductor shouldn't be overdressed in comparison to the ensemble."*

### COSTUME JEWELRY

Can enhance the ensemble image. Girls in a sophisticated, elegant costume could experiment with glittering earrings and necklaces (they must all match). Bracelets break the length and contour of the arm— not a good idea for choreography. Guys might wear matching watch chains in a vested suit (exaggerate for the zoot-suit look). As always, avoid small details that distract from clean lines and don't "read" strongly from the audience.

### DRESS UP/DRESS DOWN

Costumes can change the whole image and sound of an ensemble. An ensemble that is used to wearing off-the-rack pleated-skirts-and-a-blouse and open-shirts-with-a-vest, might keep the same style but dress "up" to bright, cartoon colors and sequins. Or, change to tuxedos and fancy dresses with a "conservatively daring" neckline. Suddenly the look is more mature and sophisticated. On a young-sounding, young-looking group, the high-heels and tuxes can have the opposite effect— they look like they are playing make-believe dress-up in Grandma's attic; even *less* mature. Dress to match your image.

*"Costumes can change the whole image and sound of an ensemble."*

## Costumes

### EYEGLASSES

Glasses create a barrier between you and your audience. They hide your eyes, they reflect light in odd ways, they slip down your nose and become a necessary part of your personal, selfish "choreography." If it is possible not to wear your glasses *safely*, don't wear them on stage. If you must wear glasses, avoid dark, heavy frames and tinted lenses or those that darken in sunlight/stagelight. Dark glasses can be fun for a special effect or novelty, but *never* as a personal fashion or cultural statement— not even in your band.

### FOUNDATION GARMENTS

Necessary. Required.

### LAUNDRY

If you invest in a set of fancy, expensive costumes, they should be laundered all together and all at the same time. Otherwise, one white shirt might come out a little pink or yellow or one of the gowns might fade a little more than the rest of the set.

### PERSONAL JEWELRY

A distraction on stage— catches and reflects light at the wrong moment in the wrong place. The *only* acceptable personal jewelry is a wedding ring. Girls with pierced ears could wear a tiny gold or silver, non-reflecting stud. The All-American look doesn't allow a guy to wear an earring on stage.

### POCKETS

Sew trouser pockets shut and cut out the extra material. Particularly in lightweight trousers, the pockets naturally sag, and because we all have the habit of going around backstage with our hands in our pockets, it doesn't take long for them to look a little extra baggy.

### QUICK CHANGE

Whether you have to change entirely from one costume to another during the show, or just add a vest or rip-off to an "under-dressed" skirt or trousers, *pre-set* the change before the show and have someone there to help with snaps (and with an emergency safety pin because the zipper *will* break!) Tape inexpensive plastic drop-cloths to the floor backstage when every second counts. The little extra pampering of having a person to act as "dresser" helps take some of the pressure and anxiety off a really quick change and allows the performer to focus on the onstage part of *The Show*.

> *"Having a person act as 'dresser' helps take some of the pressure and anxiety off a really quick change."*

## REVERSIBLE SKIRTS

So you can't afford a whole second costume. If your skirts aren't reversible, you are ignoring an entire set of skirts that you already drag to every performance and already wear in every show! The reverse can be a contrasting color, a pattern, or a flashier or specialty (country, ethnic, period) look. A wrap-around style with a velcro closure allows the quick change to take place on stage, in full view of the audience,— a terrific special effect in the middle of a high-powered dance feature!

## REVERSIBLE VESTS

In the same wardrobe case with your reversible skirts!

## SHIRT TAILS

To avoid the un-tucked, used-car salesman shirt-tail after the first high reach in your choreography, tuck your shirt-tails into your underwear; or pin them—you'll only use straight pins once! While we're on the subject, neutral, flesh-tone briefs are best under white trousers.

## SHOES

Beige shoes visually lengthen the legs of female dancers. Black, colors, and especially white add weight and attention to the feet. Boys can wear white shoes with white trousers but should otherwise wear shoes as dark as, or darker than, their trousers. For dancing, avoid dangerously high heels or delicate straps. Uniformity, practicality, and safety override "high fashion" considerations. Always build into your pre-show schedule a few rehearsals in your "show shoes!"

## SKIRT LENGTH

Ideally, each measured equally *from the floor* to create an even hemline all across the stage. Remember, we see the ensemble as one unit, not as individuals.

*"You can spot a cheerleader a mile away! Your show costumes should serve the same purpose."*

## STAGE LOOK

You can spot a cheerleader a mile away! She is dressed for a purpose. She is set apart. She is important. She has an identity. She wouldn't be caught dead in that dress style except on game days! Athletes' uniforms, too, are designed (besides function) to impart in players and fans the idea of purpose and identity. Your show costumes should serve the same purpose. A bunch of kids who "happened to wander in to sing" become "performing entertainers!" On stage your students become bigger-than-life characters; they shouldn't be dressed for fifth period Geography.

## Costumes

Bear in mind that your costumes should be *flattering* to nearly everyone, not just attractive on the store mannequin, and certainly never *un*flattering to anyone. In addition to the look, think *function*: High fashion shoes are impractical if you can't dance in them. Tapered jackets that restrict movement may look great, but they are impractical, too. Skirts, shirts, jackets that must be dry-cleaned after every wearing, or trousers that wrinkle *during* your opening number don't make sense as *costumes*!

### SUNTAN

If you decide to dress your girls in anything that is off-the-shoulder or has an open back, they need to be careful to avoid suntan lines that don't match the costume. An extreme tan looks grotesque under colored stage lights.

### UNDERDRESS

Sometimes a costume change has to happen so fast that there is only time to take *off* a pair of pants. Don't forget to wear two pair in the preceding song or scene. Underdressing works, but can be cumbersome or uncomfortable, so is practical only for a real quick-change.

### WRINKLES

*"For many groups your costumes are the only stage dressing you've got."*

Never sit in your costume. For many groups your costumes are the *only* stage dressing you've got— no curtains; no lights; no scenery; just the clothes you wear. The audience deserves to see you looking your best. When you sit down, jackets wad-up in the back, skirts crease; blouses come untucked; trousers wrinkle behind the knee. Always hang up your costume immediately and properly as you change clothes.

# 7. PUBLICITY

Short-range publicity *encourages* people to sample your product and *reminds* them how, where, and when they can do it. Advertising cannot actually *sell* your product; it can only convince prospective consumers to try it once to see if they like it. An excellent product *sells itself* to all those who give it a try. The long-range success of your program ultimately depends, not on a flashy ad campaign, but on *quality*—appealing repertoire, tight pacing and sharp visual effects that complement excellent aural effects. So much time and effort and heart go into your productions, its a shame to play to a single empty seat!

## BUDGET

Eight to ten percent of the budget is a standard amount spent for publicity and promotion. The actual amount *you* spend will depend on how much name and image recognition you need to build, how much you need to broaden the base of your support, and the size and nature of the market you are in. In a rural area, where yours is the only show in town, general scatter-shot promotion— a brief announcement in the weekly paper and a few posters on Main Street— will get the word out to everyone. The purpose of your publicity campaign is to lend an air of "Show Biz" to your overall image. In a city, you'll want to gear your advertising to reach a narrow target market, for instance, ads in selected "Neighborhood" sections of the metropolitan newspaper, not in every copy of every edition.

*"Eight to ten percent of the budget is a standard amount spent for publicity and promotion."*

## CALENDAR

Devise a publicity schedule that will maintain a more-or-less continuous exposure of your event over a three or four week period. News releases, posters, tickets, even the first drafts of the printed program, can be prepared long before the crush of rehearsals and production meetings. Prominently post your calendar in or near the rehearsal area— it will lend an air of organization, urgency, and "campaign" to your promotion.

## FREE ADVERTISING

Broadcast media are required to air a certain number and variety of "public service" announcements. Let them know about YOUR event! Also find and use media for reaching more narrowly targeted markets: community events calendars, bank and restaurant signs, church bulletins and newsletters, service club newsletters, call-in radio interview shows, publicity stunts, and, of course, news releases.

Dream up TEN ideas; with any luck FIVE of those might work out, and at least TWO ought to be terrific! (If you start with just two, one might not come through for you and the other will surely be a disaster!)

### NEWS RELEASE

*"An excellent product sells itself to everyone who will give it a try."*

The purpose of a news release isn't only to get your message to the public *through* the media— it's also to get the information *to* the media! A gentle barrage of information at regular intervals just might prompt an editor to send someone out to see what you're up to. Try to establish a *personal* contact at each media office— someone to whom you can hand-deliver really important releases. (It might be true that the editor will pay more attention when the paper's own advertising representative recommends *your* release because "They pay to advertise in our paper.")

You'll need to be aware of deadlines and length limitations and special requirements, but most media accept a standard format:

1) The heading must identify the contact-person who is responsible for the release— name, title, address, phone— and the release date or "For Immediate Release."

2) You may supply a five or six word headline, but be aware that editors often write their own headlines, so yours simply serves to introduce your release.

3) Double or triple-space with wide margins all around (for ease in editing.) Type on one side only of standard 8 1/2 x 11 paper. (Note: the use of colored paper just might draw attention to your release in a pile of fifty others.)

4. A standard news release contains One or Three-or-More paragraphs, never only two. I don't know why. The *first* paragraph should include the "Five W's": WHAT— the name of your show, WHEN— the date and time, WHO— your groups and guest artist, WHERE— place (and directions or general location), WHY— a benefit, or opening of the season, or "home" tour concert, and finally HOW— information for obtaining tickets.

5. End first pages with — MORE— and the final page with — 30— or with — ###— or with — END— .

Don't be disappointed if everything you write doesn't appear in print. Expect it. Remember, you're trying to reach the Editors, so include ALL the information and "hype" what you want, and let *them* edit!

## PAID ADVERTISING

Paid advertising will certainly give your Special Event an aura of excellence and heightened expectation. Make use of newspapers (the Entertainment section), magazines, radio (ask about quality standards if you make your own 10 and 30 second spot announcements for broadcast), billboards, bus and taxi signs, bumper stickers, posters and handbills, T-shirts, hats, balloons, and, of course, an attractive announcement to your mailing list of Core Audience. (see pg. 40)

## PHOTOGRAPHS

*Action* catches attention – (the primary purpose of a publicity picture), and directs the casual browser to the accompanying caption or article. The action in your photos can be actual or implied: a big choreography pose, conducting, singing from a copy of music, painting a backdrop, looking at a poster, accepting a donation, discussing tour arrangements.

1) For publication, black and white glossy is the standard — at least 5 x 7 inches.
2) An attached caption should identify everyone (left to right) and briefly describe the action.
3) Be sure to include your name and address on the back of every photo.
4) As a rule, no more than four people should be prominent; the action of the few *represents* the action of many: We see one pretty girl smiling and singing and *infer* that the whole crowd is doing the same. Even though everyone is singing and smiling when a large group shot is taken (looks great in person), when it is printed in the newspaper we see lots of little ants (no one is doing anything recognizable.)

*"Action catches attention – (the primary purpose of a publicity picture)."*

Sometimes you'll have to use a résumé photo (a "mug-shot"). The idea is to project *you*— your face and personality— *directly* to whomever looks at the photograph. Beware the yearbook photographer who insists on the "debutante" pose that projects one bare shoulder and a cascade of hair; lighting that reveals only one eye, cheek bones, and pouting lips; or a line of focus that implies something interesting-but-bittersweet happening somewhere off over the viewer's shoulder! Look straight into the lens (not the viewfinder), project your personality, then have the picture cropped to sell *you*, not your fashionable outfit or the atmospheric backdrop. (See photos on page 20.)

## POSTERS

Eighth grade girls are a great source of cheap posters, but avoid the every-letter-is-a-flower, magic-marker/construction-paper type that is made for every Pep Club Bake Sale! Insist on a strong, readable graphic design that will stop traffic. Standard display card size is 14 x 22 inches. Black and white, red, and yellow are the best eye-catchers. Include the Five W's: WhoWhatWhenWhereWhy'nHow. Display your posters where there is lots of foot traffic— grocery store, laundromat, drug store, fast food places. The poster committee should be supplied with tape and thumb-tacks for putting posters *up*, and should plan to return to take them *down* and deliver a personal "Thank You!" once your event is over.

*"Insist on a strong, readable graphic design that will stop traffic."*

## PUBLICITY PACKET

Your show group regularly goes out into the community to perform? You need an information/publicity packet that can both *generate* engagements and *facilitate* performance arrangements. Your packet will be unique and "tailor-made" but ought to include:

1) the official name, logo, and billing of your group

2) name, title, address and phone of your "booking agent" (you, your Activities Director, a parent)

3) names of group members and short statements to represent their talent and diversity

4) representative thank-you letters, quotes, and reviews of your shows and your kids

5) a representative list of previous appearances

6) your stage plot and technical requirements

7) information concerning the director, music department and program, and your school

## SATURATION

Remember "3 x 3". In order for your short-range publicity to be effective, prospective consumers must be exposed to the information at least THREE TIMES in at least THREE DIFFERENT WAYS. (3 x 3 *doesn't* mean running an ad in the paper three weeks in a row!)

Driving down the street you notice: "VARIETY SHOW SATURDAY NIGHT" on the bank computer sign, but you don't catch any of the particulars, so you forget it. At the drugstore you see a poster in the window that shouts: "SATURDAY NIGHT!! LIVE ON STAGE!! TWO HUNDRED ENTERTAINERS!!" You are reminded of the bank sign and have a little more information, but you're in a hurry. You get home from the grocery store and find a colorful flyer in the bottom of the bag: "SATURDAY NIGHT: WHO! WHAT! WHERE! WHEN! WHY! HOW!" *Now* you might pin it to the refrigerator door— the all-time, ultimate, bull's-eye, successful destination for *any* publicity!! When the phone rings you just might buy a couple of tickets. "3 x 3".

## VARIED APPROACHES

Discover more than one way to "slant" your news releases and other coverage of a single event:

1) ANNOUNCEMENT: "Varsity Glee Club To Present Extravaganza"
2) CAST STORY: "Student Designer Creates New Costumes"
3) SPECIAL FEATURE: "Six Decades of Dance Highlight Spring Show"
4) OPENING NIGHT: "Tonight! Live On Stage!"
5) STILL RUNNING: "Second Week of Madrigal Dinners Near SRO"

## WORDS AND PHRASES

Develop an eye and ear for effective use of language in promotion. I get accused of using outrageous hyperbole in writing publicity copy; you should too! There is too much competition for attention and support for your potential audience to fool with something that is merely "interesting" or "fun." You need to advertise "THE MOST SENSATIONAL EXPLOIT OF THE MODERN ERA, SURPASSING ALL PREVIOUS STEPS SINCE THE CREATION OF THE HUMAN RACE!!!" Here is a list to get you started:

*"Develop an eye and ear for effective use of language in promotion."*

- accomplishments
- alive and vigorous, warmth
- an irresistible musical experience
- aspiring young performers
- astounding
- captivated young and old
- comprehensive

- concept and new look
- contemporary sounds
- dynamic organization
- fast pacing, precision choreography
- full spectrum of music
- live entertainment
- musical extravaganza
- musicianship/showmanship
- one-of-a-kind
- rapid pace and professional flair never slackened
- showcase
- show-stoppers
- this remarkable gathering
- unequalled quality
- youthful excitement, energy and freshness

*Here's an idea for putting action into a group photograph. (Looks like not everyone got the message!) The jumping people provide energy and animation, but so does the background fountain.*

# 8. PUBLIC RELATIONS

Every contact you have with your "constituents" is an opportunity to shape the public perception of your program and of your performing groups. PUBLICITY, the immediate promotion of a single event, is only one facet of PUBLIC RELATIONS. You must *create* opportunities to reach out and let everyone know what's going on. You are doing great things, but if no one knows it, you're not getting the full support you need to let your program grow.

Of course, Music In Our Schools Month is a great time for general promotion of your music program, but your local community out-reach must be *on-going* and *last all year:*

*"You must create opportunities to reach out and let everyone know what's going on."*

1) APPEAR IN PERSON, regularly, before your administration and school board with substantive evidence (pictures, letters, posters, recordings— better yet, the singers themselves!) of the *success* of your program. Go ahead, ask for three minutes on the School Board agenda, then, when you are recognized, burst through the door with a piano and fifty kids in costume who can sing and dance on the tables!

2) Organize, reorganize, or build a fire under an ADULT SUPPORT GROUP— "Music Boosters"— whose sole purpose is to buy tickets and fill seats at every event during your season.

4) Arrange an INFORMAL DISCUSSION of your goals and methods with an influential member of the School Board, or the PTA President, or the director of your local arts council. Don't ask for anything specific, just let them know that you exist and that you earnestly desire their moral support.

5) Have a FACT SHEET or BROCHURE ready to mail or hand to *anyone* who'll take it. I can't stress enough the positive effect of something *physical*— something to hold, to glance at, to read— in establishing the *fact of your existence* in people's minds.

## BROAD APPEAL

You know the value of the quality literature you sing. At the end of each year you will have sung at least one representative work from each historical style period and in four languages besides English. Good for you! Job well done! The problem is that the Lion's Club President doesn't care much about "performance practice" and "The Classics." You need to show *him* that you sang for the Nursing Home at Easter, answered the phones for the local Telethon (you sang, too, didn't you?), and entered that funny float in the Pioneer Days Parade.

*Community service* is his game and because *you're* involved in community service, the Lion's Club will want to support your program.

Go right ahead in rehearsals and performance and do what you've always done— you *are* doing a great job. And, by all means, point out your *artistic* achievements to Madame Secretary of the Fortnightly Beethovian Society, but don't ignore other approaches. The aims and results of your program are educational, creative, artistic, public service and even recreational. Someone you need on your side will respond to each of these approaches!

> *"A well-written, cleverly designed brochure touches people you can't reach personally."*

## BROCHURE

A well-written, cleverly designed brochure *touches* people you can't reach personally, allows your image to *linger* with those you do contact, and *elaborates* your basic message so you don't have to "bend their ear." Your brochure can be professionally printed or run-off on the photocopier, mimeograph machine, or computer. It can be picture-oriented, showing students at every level involved in a variety of musical experiences, or it can be information-oriented, with paragraphs describing your school, your program, course offerings, performing groups, personnel, repertoire, director, and booking information.

## CORE AUDIENCE

Call them Patrons, call them Angels, call them the Top Drawer Club, but call them! Who are the people you can always count on to buy a ticket and attend your shows? Identify them. Naturally, the main body of your faithful audience is the parents and families of your students, but what about parents of *former students* who just never got out of the habit of enjoying your productions? What about the local piano teacher? Other faculty members? The mechanic who sings every Sunday in his church choir? Attend to the care and feeding of this *nucleus* and go out of your way to add to their number.

Set up a table next to the box office where patrons can fill out an information card that you can analyze and keep on file. Besides name, address, and phone, you might want to know "occupation," "regular or first-time audience member," "general musical taste," "would you support our Scholarship (or New Piano, or Tour, or Costume) Fund?"

Give the core a name, or divide them up into segments— Friends of the Chorus, Director's Council, Founder's Circle, President's Society, The Honor Roll, The Guild. They don't actually *do* anything except support you financially, receive a newsletter every-so-often, and maybe attend an evening (or lunchtime, or breakfast) "Music Appreciation" gathering to have explained some of the inside scoop on the program you will present next Thursday night.

## HOUSE SEATS

Positive public relations grows one person at a time, one encounter at a time. Here's an example: No matter how fool-proof your reserved seating plan is, something could go wrong. Everything will seem perfect until the School-Board-President-and-party-of-six show up on the wrong night, or seat H23 won't fold down (or falls off its hinges!). Hold in reserve a few good seats for the Head Usher or House Manager to use in smoothing over unforeseen problems. "An ounce of prevention..."

## IDENTIFY CONSUMERS

You know who your core audience *is*, but the constituency you *want* to reach with your message of quality and excitement is much broader. It includes:

a) the students who are *in* your program— they need to feel an integral involvement in something successful
b) students *not* in your program— think of them all as "prospective singers"!
c) the faculty of your school
d) your administration— supervisor, principal, superintendent, and school board
e) parents of your students
f) parents of the students who attend your "feeder" schools
g) their children
h) the community at large

From some of these, all you ask is an AWARENESS of your program. From others you hope to elicit INTEREST, SUPPORT, even PARTICIPATION. Target each of these groups for a specific out-reach and make them *all* feel part of The Show. You simply COULDN'T HAVE DONE IT without the help of the Spanish teacher to coach that one folk song, or the Home Ec. teacher to advise on skirt length, or the Principal to contact the bus company, or the bus drivers, or the Parents to usher, or the Boyfriends to hand out the programs, or the Community for being a town that you are Proud-To-Promote-in-a-Three-Day-Good-will-Tour-of-the-State!

These days, a one-line thank-you note is unexpected, so makes a long-lasting, positive impression.

*"Positive public relations is built step by step, one day at a time, one contact at a time."*

### LETTERS TO THE EDITOR

How many times has someone come up to you after a show to say how great the music was and what a great thing it is for kids to be involved in and what a terrific job you are doing!? How many times has your response been simply, "Why, thank you."? WRONG!

Practice at home in front of the mirror so that the next time this Golden Opportunity comes knocking, your *instant* response will be "Gosh, thanks for your support! We're so proud of what we do and would love to share it with more people. Don't you agree that's a good idea? Won't you write a letter to Editor So-and-So on our behalf?"

It's nice for you to hear compliments, but they do more good when directed *away* from you. *Above* you. Praise can trickle down, but it seldom trickles up. A letter of commendation to your supervisor is likely to stall at that level, but a letter to the School Board or Superintendent will eventually pass (with self-congratulatory memos attached) down through all the levels of bureaucracy to you and your students— and onto your bulletin board for the benefit of anyone who missed it along the way !

*"Compliments do more good when directed away from you. Praise can trickle down, but it seldom trickles up."*

### LOGO

Establish a visual identity for your total program. Choose a simple graphic that will "read" well in any size— *huge* for the backdrop of your Spring Show, or *tiny* in a two-inch newspaper ad. Music symbols are used a lot, so modify symbols from their standard form. The school Mascot is probably associated with the athletic department of your school. School colors, too, have the strongest association with athletics, so don't feel limited to those in your design concepts or costumes. Use your logo *everywhere*: programs, stationery, poster, T-shirts, sweatpants, hats, costumes and props, drums, music stands— everywhere on, in, or around *everything* associated with your program.

### PRODUCT CONCEPT

By this time you realize that your program, your groups, and you, have a public image whether you know it or not. You must *take charge* of building the IMAGE *you* want to convey. Reinforce all that is good, and work to change the negative or vague. Decide the Image you want each group and your total program to have in the minds of your consumers— a few descriptive words that will leap into the mind everytime your program is mentioned. For a High School, "fresh, young, fast-paced, and enthusiastic" are good for starters. A College group might consider "innovative, sophisticated, masterful style, tradition-of-excellence." Now, every contact you have with the public needs to reinforce the Image of your Product.

## UNIQUE IDENTITY

It is boring just to go to the "Third Period Girls Choir." It is exciting to be a *member* of, to *belong* to, to be *in* the "Belle Tones!" Each ensemble deserves a unique identity which starts with a name that reflects your concept of purpose and goals. Try a brain-storming session: you know, no idea is too stupid or bizarre. It might take some time to strike just-the-right name (you think "Belle Tones" may not be it, huh?), but you get the idea!

Okay, no excuses. Sit right down and figure out what you've got—and give it a name. Find out who supports it—and exploit that interest. Decide who *ought* to support it—and go get 'em! Remember, positive public relations is built step by step, one day at a time, one contact at a time.

*"Start with a name that reflects your concept of purpose and goals."*

*Use your logo everywhere! You want people to see you coming from a mile away. Keep it simple so it will work both big — on the equipment truck, and small — on a shoulder bag.*

Editors Note: Fritz Mountford's Video Master Class, "Publicity/Public Relations For The Choral Program" is available from Hal Leonard Publishing Corporation. See Bibliography, page 147.

# II
# PREPARING
# THE SHOW

*"Fred and Ginger"*

# "Fred and Ginger"

I remember spending hour after hour rehearsing a dance duet in the style of Fred Astaire and Ginger Rogers for a one-time performance at a large hotel. The entire number lasted only about three minutes, but we rehearsed for weeks. The routine was staged to the classic music "Begin the Beguine". My partner and I were very excited. By the time the performance was upon us we had every detail exactly how we wanted it. From each little finger and from head to toe our dance was a precise one, especially since it included numerous lifts, spins and intricate foot-work. We had rehearsed with spotlights so that we would not be thrown by their distortion and we approached our starting places with great confidence. The only elements that we had not been able to rehearse with were our costumes. They were being especially designed for the production and the designer did not have them complete until just before the downbeat of the performance. We were not concerned. My costume was a basic tuxedo with extra material here and there to allow freer movement. My partner looked radiant in her all black, sequined number with a beautiful flowing skirt complete with expensive white feathers all around the hem like an accenting boa of sorts.

Checking ourselves in the dressing room mirrors we looked smashing if I do say so myself! But, not for long...

The music swelled and so did we as we entered on opposite ends of the stage, surrounded by the eager audience. They "oohed". We puffed up and glided toward each other. We spun beautifully in a traditional dance position with my partner's bare shoulders glistening under the overhead lights. I swayed. She responded. I dipped my right shoulder to pick her up as we had done so many times in the rehearsal hall. Suddenly, all I could find was skirt! I grunted. She squirmed trying to get her hip onto my shoulder where it belonged. I came up. She was up there...somehow! I couldn't tell. In fact, I couldn't breath! My mouth was full of feathers! My partner was forcing out a smile and I was coughing up ostrich down! It was downhill from there. The longest three minutes of my performing life were spent tangled in the folds of a designer gown, the audience roaring, my partner cussing, and me resolutely vowing that from now on we rehearse every element of the show!

If you don't like rehearsal you better not be in show business. You will spend much more time alone in a rehearsal room than you will in front of an applauding audience. But, rehearsal can be the most rewarding time spent on **The Art of Entertainment.** In many ways, the process is what it's all about.

> **"If you don't like rehearsal, you better not be in show business. The process is what it's all about."**

## "Fred and Ginger"

*All of us have been at a performance where it is easy to see what has been sufficiently rehearsed and what has not. You can always tell, for instance, when the microphone technique consists of the director saying "just stick it up there and sing!" You can generally surmise when the shoes are too new, the lyrics too foreign, or the paint too wet.*

*So, there's a rhyme and reason to good rehearsal technique too. With a motto that includes "don't let the seams show," here are some absolutely essential guidelines for making the most out of your practice sessions. And for your performers' sake, don't forget to try out the costumes!*

*Use rehearsal as an experimental laboratory where individuals and the whole group "weed out" the things that don't quite work. Leave several acceptable options open to allow each performer spontaneity in performance. It sure beats "practicing" repetition of a series of mindless vocal and physical "tricks!"*

# 9. VOCAL PRODUCTION

The human voice is at the center of everything we do in preparing a choral concert or show. Without beautiful songs beautifully sung, there is no *Show*. All the fancy, extra-musical gimmicks in the world won't make up for the fact of unpleasant or improper singing.

At the Waring Workshop the staff heard hundreds of "Talent Evaluation" auditions every summer. A panel of choral clinicians would hear a workshopper sing, then offer a few suggestions for continued growth. Usually, our conversations centered around improving basic techniques like breath support, intonation, placement, and articulation. I was amazed at the number of really good singers who had only a vague notion of how the voice works; they sang well naturally, but didn't have conscious control of the process. They weren't able to understand our advice because they didn't have a basic vocabulary of terms or an understanding of the "mechanics" of vocal production.

In my choral rehearsals, I began to develop a fast-paced introduction to terms and mechanics— a sort of "owner's manual" for singers— that came to be called The Cup Routine (see RESONATION, p.57), or "The Five T's of Vocal Production." It presupposes a basic, everyday knowledge of anatomy and physiology and previous discussions of posture and energy in singing.

I certainly don't think you learn to sing in an hour-long lecture/demonstration, and I don't think you can learn to teach voice by reading a book. This is simply a suggestion of the bare-bones information every singer should know, and a few experiences and demonstrations to make the explanation vivid.

*"The human voice is at the center of everything we do. Without beautiful songs beautifully sung, there is no Show."*

## RESPIRATION

Spelling it out on the chalkboard: "The first of the Five T's of Vocal Production is RESPIRATION. What is RESPIRATION?"

The class hesitates, "breathing?"

"Yes! Breathing! That's right. RESPIRATION is breathing."

A collective sigh of relief. ("Maybe this isn't going to be so hard after all.")

"You've been breathing all your life, so you ought to be an expert by now. So, what, exactly *is* breathing? If you met a visitor from Mars, and he didn't know how to breathe (but needed to very badly!), what would you tell him to do?"

"Respiration?" "Inhale?" "You just *do* it!"

The obvious answer is confidently delivered, "You suck." (Someone *always* says it; everyone *always* laughs.)

"That's not quite all, and our Martian is turning blue."

"You suck air into your lungs."

"That's it!" Again writing on the board, "LUNGS; air into your *lungs*. But how does it *work*?"

Various answers and guesses, then a small, unsure voice will venture, "something like push your diaphragm?"

"YES! Yes. DIAPHRAGM and LUNGS!" Writing it on the board, "This will be on the nine-weeks test. Every fifth grader is expected to know specific, oddly spelled Geography terms like 'isthmus' and 'peninsula,' and *you* need to know some Physiology." (trying to spell *Pfiziol...* on the board, but giving up the effort; "Some things are important and some are not.") "DIAPHRAGM and LUNGS *are* important in RESPIRATION!"

"With your fingers, find the bottom edge of your rib cage all around here. You have a dome-shaped muscle called DIAPHRAGM that is attached about here all around the sides and back. Your DIAPHRAGM is dis-attached from your ribs right here below this hard place."

*"Concentrating on a few key components leads to understanding and control."*

(The hard place is, of course, the sternum, but the *name* of the sternum isn't important in this basic introduction. Neither is the way the intercostal muscles expand the rib cage, nor the relaxation of abdominal and back muscles, nor the need for a low tongue and high palette. The entire system is very complicated and interconnected. I've found that concentrating on a *few* key components leads to understanding and control. Insisting on *all* the details of all the parts just confuses and discourages.)

"Press your fingers here in this soft place" (just below the sternum) "and vigorously say, 'Hey, Hey, Hey.' Feel the bounce. Now, hang your tongue way out on your chin like this. Now pant very fast like a dog: AHAHAHAHAHAHA. Now bounce your fingers: AHAHAHA-HAHA. Good! Now, wipe off your chin! You are feeling the bounce of the front edge of your dome-shaped DIAPHRAGM."

(Again, resist the distraction of fascinating 'epigastriumland.' *You* know this isn't really the front edge of the diaphragm, and I know it isn't, but, for your students, the physical sensation and the mental image are so *clear*. Only those who, in later years, go into Pre-Med will hate you for ignoring a layer or two!)

"Hey, Hey, Hey. Now make a dome with your hands. Put your two thumbs together and your two pinky fingers together so you can look down through the circle they form. Bend them a little more; make a circle. Now bend your other fingers and match them up so they form the framework of a dome or upside-down bowl. Be sure the edge of your bowl sits flat on an imaginary table, not up against your chest. Put the thumb-side of your dome against the soft spot. In your imagination, pass the dome *into* your chest. Feel your thumbs attach to the front-side of your backbone, and your pinkies attach to the in-side of your lowest ribs. Good! This is the position and shape of your relaxed, dome-shaped DIAPHRAGM muscle. The *resting, relaxed* position of the DIAPHRAGM is a dome."

"On top of your DIAPHRAGM muscle, held up in place by the dome, and surrounded by the rib cage, are your...? LUNGS! Of course! Two squishy bags that can hold about as much air as a couple of plastic two-liter Coke bottles. Your LUNGS just squat on top of the dome of the DIAPHRAGM, waiting for the ride to begin."

"Hold your arm out in front of you, palm up. Either arm. Palm *up.* In this position your bicep muscle is relaxed. Now, *contract* the bicep muscle. What happens, He-man?" (Everyone demonstrates a flexed bicep.) "The muscle squeezes together; it contracts. It is the job of muscles to relax and to contract. Now, let's go back to the muscle called DIAPHRAGM."

"The *relaxed* position of the dome-shaped DIAPHRAGM is this." (Again demonstrating the dome with the hands.) "Show me *your* DIA-PHRAGM. Hold it in place inside (against) your chest, under your LUNGS. Now, what happens to the shape of *this* muscle when it contracts? Again, show me with your hands. Yes, it flattens out. Let the top of your dome flatten down to the level of your thumbs. Notice that your pinkies come apart, but if they were muscle, they wouldn't. What happens to the base of your DIAPHRAGM? Obviously, it gets bigger. Again, pant like a dog and feel your fingers bounce as the DIAPHRAGM pumps air in and out of your LUNGS."

"Now then, what happens to those baggy old LUNGS when the DIAPHRAGM flattens? They just ride down, filling up the extra outside space. They expand. And what happens to the molecules of *air* in the LUNGS? The molecules rush around to fill up the extra inside space. This action creates lower air pressure in your LUNGS, so now the air out here rushes in— *pushed* by the weight, the 'pressure', of the air above and around you— into your mouth, down your throat, and into your LUNGS, until the pressure is equal inside and outside."

> *"The air out here rushes in—pushed by the weight, the 'pressure' of the air above and around you."*

"Again: Your DIAPHRAGM *contracts* to a flat position." (Show it with your hands.) "The LUNGS ride down, *expanding*, and creating extra space. Outside air rushes *into* the 'vacuum' until the pressure is equalized. Put your fingers in the soft spot and take a really deep breath. Feel the edge of your DIAPHRAGM push out as it flattens. Actually, *first* your DIAPHRAGM flattens, and *then* you get a deep breath. The air doesn't push in like blowing up a balloon; it is *drawn in* by lower air pressure. It is like the action of a fireplace bellows: You pull the handles apart which makes more space in the accordion wedge. Result: low air pressure inside, so the outside air rushes through the little spigot ready to be expelled when you push the handles back together."

"You control how much air the bellows 'inhales' by controlling the width of the handles. You control how much air *you* inhale by controlling the contraction of the DIAPHRAGM. Here's an exercise: Show me a wide, toothy smile. Say a bright, high-pitched 'EEEEE.' Hold your mouth in this position and inhale sharply. Be aware of how much (or little) air you inhale. Picture how much or little your DIAPHRAGM dome is flattening, how much or little the muscle contracts. Now say a round, relaxed, 'OHHH.' Again, hold your mouth in this position and inhale sharply. Feel how much more deeply you inhale. Your DIAPHRAGM contracts more and flattens further and allows more air into your LUNGS. It is this 'deep' breathing that you need for singing."

*"Flip the tip up and breathe around both sides of your tongue: Instant low breath!"*

("This creates quite a problem for smiling singers. You can't stop every two bars in the middle of the opening song-and-dance number to relax to an 'OHHH' while you take a deep breath. Here's a solution: Flip the tip of your tongue up as though you were going to make the sound of the letter 'T'. Now, use your tongue as a baffle and breathe *around* both sides of your tongue. Instant low breath. It works even better with your mouth in the 'EEEE' shape. Neat, huh? It may take a little practice in the bathroom with the door locked and the water running, but eventually your mouth can keep its wide, toothy grin, while you take a deep, oxygen-filled breath!")

"Let's all contract our DIAPHRAGMS together! Ready? Inhale! Do it again— show it with your hands! Could you explain it to a Martian? Drawing in air, *in*haling, is the first part of RESPIRATION. Now let's look at the second part, *ex*haling."

"Blow a cool breath against your hand." (Nearly everyone will blow through an 'OO' shaped mouth.) "Now, blow a hot breath against your hand." (The majority will exhale with a well-supported, 'HAH, HAH'.) Feel the physical difference between the shallow 'OO' and the deep 'HAH'.

"Who can tell me how it *works*?" (Hope for a general hubbub indicating focus of attention and a glimmering of understanding of *process*, not just *mechanics*.) "I think you've got the general idea: the DIAPHRAGM rises back to the dome-shaped position. It pushes up to squeeze the LUNGS, forcing air up through the throat and back out through the mouth. Very good."

"Put your hands in place to represent your DIAPHRAGM. Show the action of the DIAPHRAGM in each step of this exercise: Inhale deeply, then release the air suddenly with a whoosh— SHHHhh! Your DIAPHRAGM rises all at once, without control. Inhale again, but this time release the air through a controlled hiss— SSSSSSSSssssssss. Remember to show the controlled relaxation of the DIAPHRAGM with your hands. Take a few deep breaths, then let's use the clock to time our controlled release. Inhale and control the release— ssssssssssssssssss. Much better. You are simply controlling the relaxation of your DIAPHRAGM."

"In a conversational tone and volume, say the alphabet: A, B, C, D, E, F, G, H, etc... How far do you get on one breath? Try it again, but *control* your DIAPHRAGM: A, B, C, D, E, F, G, H, I, J, K, L, etc... When you concentrate, you go further, right? Don't forget to keep breathing between the exercises! Now, let's do it again, but this time hold your palm about an inch in front of your mouth and be aware of which letters, which sounds, blow a puff of 'wasted' air against your hand: A, B, C, D, — Excuse me, but speak at the same pitch and volume levels you used before." (The solution is *not* to get suddenly soft and energy-less!) "Again: A, B, C, D, E, F, G, H, I, J, K, L, M, N, O, P, Q, R, etc...let's make a list on the board of those that puff air. Tell me which ones? 'B, S, T, K, F, L' — does 'L' puff air? No? Okay, let's go ahead." (Continuing the list in no particular order; another time it might be interesting to categorize which sounds puff against the palm — P, T, H, etc. — and which ones puff against the fingers — F, V, etc.) "Finally say the alphabet a last time, but concentrate on not puffing extra air. *Control* the relaxation of your DIAPHRAGM; A, B, C, etc."

"Now hear this:"

"Exhalation is the part of RESPIRATION we use in making sound. In order to exhale, the DIAPHRAGM must rise to the *relaxed* position. Exhalation is a process of relaxation. SINGING IS CONTROLLED RELAXATION. This is important. Teachers urge you to sing with energy. They are right. However, in trying to explain the source of singing energy, many teachers urge you to 'push' from the DIAPHRAGM. I think they are wrong; at least they mislead you. It *is* vigorously exhaled air that delivers energy to your singing system, but your DIAPHRAGM is in the process of *relaxing* just at the moment you need to generate *more* energy. Where does the energy, the *push*, come from? How does it work?"

"Is there anyone here who has never vomited? Good! Stand up and gag! Everybody together, 'H—!'" (I can't imagine how to spell it, but everyone will know the sound *and* the sensation!) "Careful; I don't want the real thing, just an approximation! 'H—!' You've been practicing. Now, here is where my belly-button is. Show me yours. No,

*"Exhalation is a process of relaxation. Singing is controlled relaxation."*

no! Show me *where* it is! Press your fingers down here below your navel and gag. 'H—!' Feel what happens? It happened before, but not so dramatically, when we exhaled a hot breath, 'HAH'. Feel it? Your LOWER ABDOMINAL MUSCLES contract." Writing on the chalkboard, "Add this to your list: DIAPHRAGM, LUNGS, and LOWER ABDOMINAL MUSCLES. Hard as a rock, right? Imagine a rock." Suddenly, Mister Rogers' Neighborhood:

"Hello, neighbor.

"Will you be my neighbor?

"Can you imagine a rock?

"Imagine a rock with me right now.

"Make a fist with your left hand and imagine it is a rock. Imagine how it feels: hard and irresistible.

"Now imagine a cotton handkerchief.

"Shake your loose right hand and imagine it is a white cotton handkerchief. Imagine how *it* feels: soft and flexible, relaxed.

"Gently drape the handkerchief over the rock. Cover the rock with the handkerchief.

"In your imagination, touch the cloth-covered rock.

"Which do you feel more? The softness of the handkerchief, or the hardness of the rock?

"Which do *you* feel, neighbor?

"That's right; you feel the hardness of the rock *through* the soft handkerchief.

"Thank you, neighbor. I'm happy that you're my neighbor."

"You feel the *rock* through the handkerchief. The hardness exerts its character even through the soft layer. In exhaling, your DIAPHRAGM is relaxing, becoming like the handkerchief— not exerting much energy on the system. Where, then, is the energy? What is the rock?"

> *"You're standing around with a plate in one hand, a cup in the other, and a mint in your mouth."*

"Picture the wide and thick ABDOMINAL MUSCLES that crisscross down here below your belly-button. When they contract, they exert a sort of in-and-up pressure on all your giblets. The muscles of your buttocks do the same. You know this gimmick: 'You're standing around at a wedding reception balancing a plate of cake in one hand, a cup of punch in the other, and a mint in your mouth. Someone comes up to you and says, "Here, hold this dime for me." Where is the obvious place to put it?' ...That's right! Everybody in unison, Squeeze Your Cheeks! 'TENSE YOUR BUTTOCKS NOW!' Hold that dime! Smile! This feeling becomes important in generating the energy for singing. Both in front and in back, these low, heavy muscles push in-and-up ('Tip, Tuck, and Tighten'), which puts a rock solid foundation for the viscera (you know, stomach and liver and intestines and whatever else is compacted in there) to transfer the energy to your relaxing DIAPHRAGM."

"RESPIRATION is easy: pant like a dog to find your DIA-PHRAGM, use your tongue as a baffle behind a toothy grin to fill your LUNGS, then vomit and squeeze your cheeks to activate LOW AB-DOMINAL support! At contest, every choir should be *required* to file slowly onto the risers, slowly raise their music folders, focus intently on the conductor, then suddenly Pant-Grin-Gag-Squeeze before they sing! Suggest this to your director at school or church."

## PHONATION

"The second of Five T's of Vocal Production is PHONATION." Writing on the chalkboard, "PHONATION is simply the vibration of your *vocal cords* in your *larynx*. This will be on the test: VOCAL CORDS and LARYNX. Learn to spell and pronounce LARYNX correctly!"

"Hold up your index finger. Either hand. Up. Now place the tip of your finger right here at the front of your throat on your Adam's Apple." (Some sopranos and most students with unchanged voices may need to throw the head back, stretching the throat, in order to locate the small bump that is the front of the larynx.) "Use your index finger and thumb to feel the front side of a bumpy tube. The tube you feel is your LARYNX. Your Adam's Apple is the top front edge of that tube. Don't jam your finger in there, but gently find the little V-shaped notch that spreads up and back from your Adam's Apple. Your two little VOCAL CORDS are attached to your LARYNX just inside the V-shaped notch. They are both hooked to the same spot in front. In back they attach to two separate, moveable thingies that spread apart to form a V-shaped opening or come together so the edges of your two VOCAL CORDS touch."

"Touch your index finger to the V. I want everyone to sustain a long SSSSSS then, when I snap my fingers, change the SSSSSS to ZZZZZZ. Ready, go. SSSSSS / ZZZZZZ! Feel it? During the 'S' the vocal cords are apart and air just rushes through. In order to make the 'Z' the cords come together and the air passing through the tube makes them flap together— your finger feels the vibration— and we hear the vibration as a pitch."

"You already know that anything that vibrates has pitch. Here is a plastic ruler, trained to do tricks." (You probably have a trained ruler, too, but you've never asked it to show off!)
"SHAKE! Good boy."
"Now, LIE DOWN! DOWN. LIE DOWN. Good boy!"
"Ready, SPEAK! SPEAK!"
"Of course he can't speak lying down; he needs to vibrate!"

*"You already know that anything that vibrates has pitch."*

(Firmly holding the ruler on the desk with about half hanging over like a diving board and giving it a good whack.)

"SPEAK! SPEAK!" (The ruler goes fwadadadadada.)

"Good boy! Now, HIGHER!"

"Come on, boy, HIGHER! SPEAK HIGHER!" (Move the ruler to shorten the length of the vibrating end and tap it again.)

"ATTA BABY! Now LOWER! SPEAK LOWER!" (Lengthen the vibrating end.)

"Good boy! That's all for today, boy."

"Now SIT! STAY!"

"Here is a rubber band. No, it doesn't do tricks. You must be crazy; you can't train a rubber band to do tricks. But it *can* vibrate and make a pitch." (Plucking the rubber band.) "Listen closely. It isn't very loud, but you can hear a pitch. If I stretch it further, the pitch goes up. Your VOCAL CORDS are small like this rubber band, but VOCAL CORDS are *flaps* of flexible tissue, not stretchy string. If you could take your VOCAL CORDS out and vibrate them, they would make a soft sound like this. Again: everything that vibrates has pitch. The vibrating rubber band has pitch and the vibrating ruler ('STAY! STAY!') has pitch. The vibration of your VOCAL CORDS in your LARYNX is called PHONATION. Let's all phonate in a group! Again: SSSSSS / ZZZZZZ."

"With your hand, show me a 'V for Victory' or 'Peace.' Now turn your hand over so the two fingers point toward you. Spread them apart, touch them together. Spread, touch. This is what your VOCAL CORDS do. Again, say SSSSSS / ZZZZZZ, but use your fingers to show the open or closed position of the VOCAL CORDS. Open, apart, for 'S' and closed, together for 'Z'. Do it on your own: SSS /ZZZZZ / SSS / ZZZZZZ / SSS. Show the contrast with your fingers while you touch your LARYNX with your other hand. Feel and see and say: SSSS / ZZZZ / SSSS / ZZZZ."

"Now, let's all phonate in unison. Vibrate with me!" (Sing an 'oo' vowel at about the pitch F above middle C— moderate for girls and an easy falsetto for most guys.) "In order to sound this pitch, our vocal cords must all vibrate at the rate of 400 times every second! How fast would you run if your *legs* could vibrate 400 times every second? (For now, don't worry about exact pitch, but '400' is an easy number to think about for this exercise.) "Keep breathing. Just sustain a unison pitch."

*"How fast would you run if your legs could vibrate 400 times every second?"*

(Some guys may sing the octave below the unison pitch.) "Oh, some of you can only vibrate at 200. Guys, *all* vibrate at 200." (They sing in their mid-range voices.) "Now, how many can vibrate at 100? 200? 100? 200? 400? Girls at 400? 800? Everyone in unison: 400." (Experiment with the concept of pitch having something to do with a mathematical relationship of vibrations-per-second.)

"What happens if I stop concentrating on 400? What is my vibration rate slips to 399 or 397 or 396? You-all keep singing 400 and let's see what happens if I get off pitch. (Most students will be able to hear or feel the 'beats' as one voice slips away from unison.) "Now let me slide below, then back up to 400, then slightly above, and finally back to unison 400. You-all sustain 400. Breathe when you need to!"

"Everyone choose a partner. One of you be 'A' and the other 'B'. Start singing unison 400— really match a perfect unison. You may need to modify the 'oo' vowel a little until you are really vibrating in unison. Now, while 'A' holds 400, let 'B' slip a few beats to 399 or 397 or 396. Feel the beats! Make them slower and faster. Then climb back up to perfect unison. Good! Now let 'B' hold onto 400 while 'A' sings 401, 402, 403. Feel the pull. Return to unison. Keep breathing."

"I want you to be aware of how *much* energy and concentration it takes to climb up to 401, 402, 403; and how much energy it takes to climb back up to 400 once you've slipped below it. On the other hand, be aware of how easy it is to slip below the pitch. Your concentration flags just for a moment and your vibration rate changes enough for the 'beats' to happen. The difference between 400 and 395 beats per second is really miniscule, but it's the difference between singing in-tune and out-of-tune. When everyone phonates in true unison you can almost feel the lights get brighter and the temperature in the room get cooler and fresher. PHONATION is simply controlling the vibration of your VOCAL CORDS in the LARYNX. The adjustments are very minor and call for tremendous mind control. It really is true that singing is 99% thinking!"

*"When everyone phonates in true unison, you can feel the lights in the room get brighter!"*

## RESONATION

"Do you sing in the shower? Did you ever notice that, as you're singing, one certain pitch is suddenly louder and richer sounding? Experiment in stairwells and restrooms— anyplace that is relatively enclosed and has lots of hard surfaces that will reflect sound. Walk into a large room and clap your hands sharply. Some rooms echo the high 'ping' of the sound, while some seem to soak it right up. Various spaces are naturally 'in tune' to certain pitches. If you change the shape of your shower stall, even slightly, you would change the certain pitch that will echo best in that space. Different shaped spaces naturally 'resonate' different pitches."

"Listen to what happens when I take my little rubber band that represents a vibrating vocal cord and stretch it across the mouth of a

# Vocal Production

paper cup." Plucking it a few times. "It gets louder and has a more 'musical' tone. All I've done is to create a little shower stall around the vibrating pitch source. What is the shower stall that amplifies and colors the sound of your vibrating vocal cords? Let's find out."

"Whisper these vowel sounds all in one breath." Writing on the board: oo oh ah ay ee. "Whisper the sounds. No phonation, no vocal cord vibration, just whispered air. All together: oo oh ah ay ee. Do you hear the pitch rise? Whisper again! Put your finger against your larynx to feel that your vocal cords aren't vibrating. But we *do* hear pitch, so *something* is vibrating. Right! The *air* is vibrating and the pitch changes as the shape of your mouth changes!"

"The third of Five T's of Vocal Production is RESONATION. RESONATION is the coloring and amplification of vocal sound. RESONATION takes place in your MOUTH, THROAT, and NASAL CAVITY. By altering the shape and size of these little echo chambers, you alter the character of the basic sound made by the vibration of your tiny vocal cords. Your shower stall can't change shape, so it amplifies only one or two pitches. You *can* change the shape of your resonating cavities, so you can amplify a wide variety of pitches. The *best* vocal sound happens when the spaces change shape ever-so-slightly to best agree with each individual pitch created by the vocal cords."

"Individual singers can produce a wide variety of tone colors. Individual instruments can't. The reason is that most instruments have a fixed shape. The echo chamber is frozen forever in a shape that makes only an 'ee' vowel sound or only an 'oh' vowel sound. What vowel sound does an oboe make? ee? What about a french horn? oh? Think about the characteristic vowel sound of a bassoon: rr? In your imagination, play the 'ee' on your oboe. Now magically begin to bend the oboe. Make its resonating cavity slightly thicker and shorter. Hear the sound change from 'ee' to 'ih'. Sounds more like a clarinet doesn't it? An instrumentalist needs two different instruments to make 'ee' and 'ih'. A singer makes both 'ee' and 'ih' and countless other vowels with the same flexible instrument!"

*"By altering the shape and size of these little echo chambers, you alter the character of the basic sound."*

"Sing the vowel sound 'ee'. Now on the same pitch, sing a very dark, veiled, stupid sounding 'ee'. Again, sing the same pitch 'ee' (no change in the vibration rate of the vocal cords), but with a bright, piercing, nasal quality. All three are phonated identically in your larynx, but the shape of your THROAT, MOUTH, and NASAL CAVITY changes to make the different tone colors happen. Sustain an 'ee', but let it change character as you sustain it; start bright and nasal, then gradually make the sound change to dark and throaty. Somewhere between the too-bright and too-dark sounds is a range of tone that is acceptable and probably even beautiful. It is the job of your voice teacher or choir director to choose the sounds that are 'right' in any given instance. It is *your* job to know how to produce and reproduce the 'right' sound on command."

"Your ears are an unreliable source of information when it comes to reproducing the 'right' sound. The reason is, that, because of the way your head and face are glued together, you are always standing *behind* your voice. If you wanted to check out the sound of new stereo speakers, you wouldn't go around behind them to evaluate their sound."

"Sing a good 'ee' vowel sound on a sustained pitch. Let your teacher identify when you are creating a 'good' sound. Now, without changing the *production* of the tone, cup your hands around the back of your ears and bend them slightly forward. Do you hear the sound change? It *sounds* more like the bright, nasal tone you created by changing the shape of the resonating cavities, but you didn't change the shape at all! Find the 'good' sound again and sustain it while you cup your hands backwards in front of your ears. Fold your cupped hands back over your ears. The *sound* changes again! More like the dark, stupid tone, right? Your vocal mechanism is creating an unchanging tone, but your ears are telling you that the tone is changing. Your ears lie!"

"If you always stood in the same place, in the same room, beside the same people, you could learn to trust your ears in recreating the 'right' sound. But, chances are, you sing in a variety of settings. The only sure way of monitoring RESONATION is by *feeling* the sensations of the 'right' sound and recreating the feeling everytime you sing."

"Do the cupping-hands-over-and-behind-ears exercise again. This time, concentrate, not on the sound of your voice, but on the sensations you feel as you sustain the tone. If the *production* doesn't change, the *feeling* won't change! At first, you may think that the feeling changes, especially when you cup your hands behind your ears. Learn to differentiate between hearing and feeling! As you experiment with RESONATION, and your choral director or voice teacher identifies a variety of 'right' sounds, *memorize the feelings*."

"Form your lips into a narrow 'oo' shape. Inhale sharply. Be aware of the sound of the air rushing past your lips. Can you make minor adjustments in the shape of your lips and tongue to change the pitch? Now, I want you to learn to make the same sort of quiet sucking sound in the back of your mouth, at the top of your throat:

"Relax your tongue in your mouth. Put the tip of your tongue behind your lower front teeth. Now, curl the sides of your tongue up to touch your upper molars. You're trying to create a tunnel that will channel air back to your uvula. Didn't you know that little floppy

*"Your ears are an unreliable source of information when it comes to reproducing the 'right' sound. As your teacher identifies a variety of 'right' sounds, memorize the feeling."*

# Vocal Production

*"Didn't you know that little floppy thingie had a name? Say it fast: UvulaUvulaUvula!"*

thingie had a name? Say it fast: UvulaUvulaUvula! Rrrrr. Everyone twirl your uvula! Inhale gently to make the sucking sound, not with your lips but back here where you gag yourself with your toothbrush. Feel the spot that gets cold and dry as you continue to inhale. You can't really feel the change in shape, but when you inhale against that spot, the roof of your mouth rises to change the shape of the back of your throat. At home, get a good look at your uvula in the mirror, then inhale with a little gasp as though you were suddenly startled. You'll see your SOFT PALETTE rise to an arch shape."

"Make the sucking sound again and feel the cold, dry spot. Touch the spot with the incoming air. Now, sing a gentle 'oo' and, in your imagination, touch the same spot with the outgoing sound. Relax the sides of your tongue away from your upper teeth, but keep the arch of your PALETTE. By making a rounder, more elegant echo chamber out of your mouth and throat, you are able to make a rounder, richer, more elegant vocal sound."

"When I talk about changing the shape of your MOUTH, I don't mean just the shape of your lips. You can change the shape of your tongue and cheeks (close your lips and move your jaw up and down and around) to change the *inside* shape of your mouth. Moving the back of your tongue and your palette (watch in the mirror) changes the shape of your THROAT. Make a difference between your neck (outside) and your throat (inside).

The reason I talk about NASAL CAVITY instead of 'nose' is so you'll think about what goes on deep *inside*, not just at your nostrils." "Put the tip of your tongue up behind your upper teeth. Now sustain an 'nnn' sound. Change the shape of your MOUTH, THROAT, and NASAL CAVITY to make the 'nnn' brighter and darker. Focus your concentration on the sensation created by the bright 'nnn'. You should feel a little tingling around your eyes and across the bridge of your nose. It will be an *inner* sensation more than a vibration you can feel with your fingers against your face. This feeling is a result of MASK RESONANCE; think of the bony structure around your eyes and across your nose like a raccoon's mask. Experiment with placing the 'nnn' in and out of the MASK."

(Some singers feel RESONANCE better using a round 'mmm' and still others feel it best using 'vvv'. Use what works!)

"Now let's try to transfer the sensation of MASK RESONANCE from the 'nn' to the vowels. Find the 'right' feeling of 'nnn', then slowly drop the tip of your tongue away from the roof of your mouth to make the vowel 'ee'. Try to keep the sensation of tingle or buzz in the MASK. It won't be as as strong, but you will be able to feel it. Now sing 'nnneennneennnee', keeping the sensation of MASK RESONANCE. The vowel may sound nasal and ugly to you, but remember that you can't trust your perception of the *sound* of your voice. Let your teacher tell you when the sound is right, while you memorize, and be able to recreate, the *feeling* of your voice."

"Next try singing 'nnneennnaynnneennnaynnnee'. Really use the 'nnn' to establish the sensation of RESONANCE. 'EE' and 'AY' will probably be the easiest for you to transfer the sensation. Eventually, you'll be able to transfer a beautiful, resonant tone through 'nee, nay, nah, noh, noo' all on one pitch. At the same time, try 'nee, nee, nee' on two or three adjacent pitches. The idea is to modify the resonating cavities ever-so-slightly so that the sound of each next vowel and each next pitch 'match'. Trained singers spend their lives perfecting the ability to make the sound of *every* vowel and *every* pitch match. In order to do this, they must memorize thousands of minute variations of the sensation of MASK RESONANCE. They pay voice teachers and coaches really big bucks to be their 'ears,' to tell them when the sound is 'right.'"

"Say this in quick rhythm: 'oneandtwoandthreeandfourand'. Now accent the 'and': 'oneANDtwoANDthreeANDfourAND'. Be aware of the *energy* that goes into accenting the 'AND'. Say, 'ooAHooAHooAH-ooAAAAH.' Same accent. Now say, 'niNEhunDREDnineTYniNEnuNs-iNterNEdinANinDIaNANunNEry'! Come on, in rhythm! 'Nine hundred ninety nine nuns interned in an Indiana nunnery!' Give energy and length to every accented 'nnn.' Chant it on a medium pitch. Feel the resonant character of 'nnn' carry over to every vowel sound."

(For *most* singers, the sensation of resonance is felt in the mask. For some, the sensation of vibration is strong in the chest. And, of course, knowing that the vibrating source of the sound is in the throat, some will try to locate the "controllable" sensation there. The danger of trying to control *chest* sensation is, among other things, that it isn't consistent throughout the entire range of the voice. Almost any attempt to control *throat* sensation will lead to a constricted mechanism. (Can you think of Dudley Doright's cartoon voice? Or Gomer Pyle's trademark "Gol-ly"? Pee-Wee Herman?) On the other hand, don't confuse mask resonance with nasal singing. It may *feel* nasal to an untrained singer, but the teacher's ears must be the final judge.)

(As a matter of fact, there is evidence that the high overtones we hear as resonance are actually created immediately above the vocal cords. I expect that there are too few of the right sort of nerve endings there for us to be conscious of the infinitesimally fine motor control needed to modify shape at that level!)

*"Singers spend their lives perfecting the ability to make every vowel and every pitch match."*

"So, RESONANCE is controlled by modifying the shape of your built-in echo chambers, the MOUTH, THROAT, and NASAL CAVITY. As an entertainer, you'll want to paint a wide variety of colors and moods and stories for your audience. Think of changes in tone color, RESONATION, as the 'facial expressions' of your voice!"

## ARTICULATION

"In our discussion of Vocal Production so far, we've talked about things that every music making machine has in common. Now we get to the element that really sets singers apart. RESONATION creates all the colors of the various vowel sounds. In fact, each vowel is nothing more than a family of closely related sounds that sound just about the same. Think of the nasal 'ee' and the stupid 'ee;' they are really two *different* sounds, but close enough that we agree to give them the same name: 'E'. RESONATION creates vowels.

"Every infant who has experimented with creating sounds knows that it is possible to interrupt or interfere with the steady flow of vowel sound. It doesn't take long for a baby to progress from 'oo' and 'oh?' and 'ee!' to 'goo' and 'bubububuh' and 'mamamamamah' and even 'vvvsh'. Baby is discovering certain combinations of TEETH, TONGUE, and LIPS that make satisfying alterations in the sounds of the vowels. Baby has stumbled upon the fourth of Five T's of Vocal Production, ARTICULATION!

"Using your knowledge of RESPIRATION, PHONATION, and RESONATION, make a steady stream of 'ah' vowel. Now use your lips to interfere with the sound. Press your lips together: 'mmm'. Congratulations, Baby! You've just invented consonants! ARTICULATION creates consonants. Sing 'ah' again, but this time cause the interference with just your lower lip and your upper teeth: 'vvv'."

"Now try your *upper* lip and your *lower* teeth: oops! Well, that's a consonant, too; it's just that we don't often use it in a meaningful way, so we don't have a symbol to represent the sound. Try using just your teeth: 'zzz'. Now, tongue and teeth: 'th'. Those sounds are just as stupid, but for some reason we've decided to keep them and give them meaning and symbols: 'Z' 'TH'. Here's one that Baby discovers about the same time as he discovers creamed peas: Sing 'ah' again, then stick your tongue way out. Now close your loose lips around your tongue to create: 'motorboatmotorboatmotorboat'!! Another really useful consonant sound that we don't use in everyday speech!"

"So far, our consonants have just interfered with the vowel flow. Now let's see if we can totally *interrupt* the vowels. Sing 'ah' again, then abruptly flip the tip of your tongue up behind your upper teeth. The vowel sound stops, so we must have a consonant. Do we have a symbol for it? Again, flip your tongue up and blow a puff of air. As your tongue comes away from behind your teeth we hear a sound we've agreed to represent by the symbol 'T'. Interrupt 'ah' again with 't' and we hear: 'aht'. Now there's a combination with meaning! (Somebody decided we ought to spell it 'OUGHT', but you ought to understand it however it is spelled.)"

"As a matter of fact, you ought to know it even if my tongue flips up to stop the vowel without flipping back down to puff 'T'. Say: 'you ought to know it.' In the written symbols you *see* 'T' three times, but when you say it, do you *hear* 'T' three times? 'you oughT To know iT.' Sounds a liT-Tle peculiar doesn'T iT? Perhaps you hear 'T' only once, at the beginning of the word 'To'. At the end of 'ought' and at the end of 'it', you may simply *stop* the vowel without actually making the sound of the consonant. We still understand what you are saying."

"The reading of written language symbols is a different process from the hearing of spoken (or sung) language symbols. Reading and hearing are different. Writing and speaking are different. You understand me whether or not I sound the 'T' at the end of 'ought'. In fact, you would probably *misunderstand* me if I suddenly decided to sound the 'GH' in the middle of 'ought'!! Written language and spoken language are different."

"This concept of the *purpose* of ARTICULATION is important for entertainers, because we are interested in getting the message of the words across to the audience in the most natural way. Just as we can control the 'quality' of the sound by controlling RESONATION, we can control the 'flavor' of the sense of the message by controlling ARTICU-LATION. As a singer, you need to have conscious control of your TEETH, TONGUE and LIPS all the time. Otherwise you end up with strange sounds that have no meaning. You can even end up with familiar sounds that have no meaning!"

> *"The reading of written language symbols is a different process from the hearing of spoken language symbols."*

## PERSPIRATION

"At long last we come to the fifth of Five T's of Vocal Production."
Beginning to write on the board: 'PE', but pausing to say,
"We've discovered that RESPIRATION is the process that allows your DIAPHRAGM to pump air in and out of your LUNGS. Now, you control how much air goes in and how much goes out. You control the volume of your singing and the length of the phrases you sing. You control the clarity and freedom of well-supported singing."
"The first T, RESPIRATION, is important, but not as important as the fifth T."
Continuing to write: 'PER'...
"You know, the second T, PHONATION, is crucial to good

# Vocal Production

singing, too. By controlling the vibration rate of your VOCAL CORDS in your LARYNX you can choose to sing in-tune or out-of-tune. You can be sensitive to matching pitch *exactly* in unison singing, and you can feel the 'rightness' of the mathematical balance when you sing your part of a chord."

More dramatically, leading the class on tongue-in-cheek:

Yes, indeed, PHONATION is important, but the *fifth* T..."

Writing 'PERS'...

"Come to think of it, the third T, RESONATION is where all the beauty is created. You use your echo chambers, the MOUTH, THROAT, and NASAL CAVITY to amplify and color the sounds you make. *You* can choose to paint with bright, vivid, spirited sounds. You can choose to paint with dull, lifeless, disinterested sounds. You choose a narrow range or a broad range of tone colors. I really like to play with RESONATION. It is what makes the sound of a choir unique in all the world!"

"Number five tops it, though..."

Turning as if to write, but stopping.

"No, no. Number four, ARTICULATION is my favorite. As long as I'm in the business of communicating *ideas*, I want to be able to use language to get the ideas across. Fred Waring taught me to sing 'All the beauty of all the sounds of all the syllables of all the words.' You can use your TEETH, TONGUE and LIPS to be sure that the audience gets the message of every song. After all, it is the *words* that make a song; otherwise, it's just a melody."

Writing 'PERSPI...'

"You could spend a lifetime learning about RESPIRATION, PHONATION, RESONATION, and ARTICULATION. Lots of people do. In fact they are really committed to the fifth of Five T's of Vocal Production."

At long last, finishing 'PERSPIRATION'.

*"If you're going to get up on stage, you have to know you've given everything you've got to being the best you can be."*

"That's right! PERSPIRATION is on the list to remind you to *work* at singing beautifully. *Work* at singing meaningfully. *Work* at developing your voice. *Work* at sharing your talent every chance you get. If you're going to get up on stage in front of an audience and expect them to pay attention to what you are doing, you have to know that you've given everything you've got to being the best you can be. Without PERSPIRATION, you can never hope to control the other elements of Vocal Production."

Editor's Note: Fritz Mountford's Video Master Class "Vocal Production" is available from Hal Leonard Publishing Corporation. See Bibliography, p.147

# 10. COMMUNICATION AND INTERPRETATION

## SUCCESSFUL COMMUNICATION

I have an idea! This:  ✳

is a picture of my idea. It could be a big idea or a little idea. In order for my idea to be meaningful to you, I need to transfer the idea from my brain to your brain:

I can write it, sign it, send smoke signals, or even sing it.

In order for that to happen, something must first happen in my brain. I need to translate my idea into symbols— written symbols, hand symbols, smoke symbols, or speech symbols.

Once I've chosen a particular set of symbols, I need to send them to you:

I can write on paper and mail you the symbols, or save them in the computer for you to retrieve. I can make signs and facial expressions (in person, on live TV, or by prerecorded video) that you can see. I can utter a variety of sounds (again— in person, either face-to-face or around the corner, or by phone/radio/video around the world and across time.) The only trick is that you must have some way of hearing the sounds. By sight, sound, or any other sense, it is vital that you be able to *receive* the symbols I send.

Now, *your* brain needs to translate the symbols you receive:

Hopefully, you end up with an idea that matches my original:  ✳

If my  ✳  equals your  ✳ , then we've experienced *successful communication!*

Here, then, is a picture of *successful* communication:

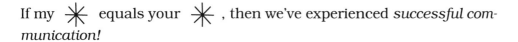

> *"To transfer the idea from my brain to yours, it is vital that you be able to receive the symbols I send."*

# Communication and Interpretation

Successful communication *seems* easy. 1) I get an idea. 2) I "encode" the idea into symbols. 3) I send the symbols to you. 4) You receive the symbols. 5) You "decode" the symbols. 6) You understand the idea. Easy. *I* do 123, *you* do 456.

But what if I choose a set of symbols you don't understand? *Parlez vous Francais?* Morse — • — •   — — —   — • •   • ? What if the sun emits solar flares in the middle of my sending? What if your daughter runs to the TV screen to give my image a big, smeary peanut butter and jelly kiss? (Read my lips.) What if your computer isn't set to receive my mail message? What if my castaway SOS-in-a-bottle is swallowed by a whale? My ✳ won't be the same as your ✳ ! *Unsuccessful* communication. Here is a picture of unsuccessful communication:

> *"Anything that interferes with successful communication has the technical name 'Noise'."*

Anything that interferes with ✳ = ✳ has the technical name "Noise".

"Noise" may be sound, but it doesn't have to be. "Noise" can be aural or visual or cultural or psychological or cosmic. "Noise" can happen at any stage of the *production* end of communication:

or at any stage of the *perception* end of communication:

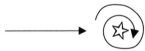

"Noise" is the cause of everything from minor differences between the produced idea and the perceived idea to major misunderstandings:

> Oldest joke in the book:
> Three little old ladies riding an open streetcar.
> Number one says, "Let's get off at the next stop; I think it's windy."
> Number two says, "No, dear, it's Thursday."
> Number three says, "Oh, does she want a drink?"
> Number one says, "I told you what I think! It's *windy*!"
> Number two, "It's *Thursday*!"
> Number three, "Well, I am too! Let's get off at the next stop!"

Successful communication! Sometimes a lot of hard work!

### COMMUNICATION IN ENTERTAINMENT

Entertainment is audience oriented. The idea is for communication to happen without all the hard work. Entertainers are greatly concerned with the "perception" side of communication. What does the *audience* understand? Do they get the message? Of course much is often made of the "production" side— it can be innovative and exciting and expensive, but if the audience doesn't get the message, there is *no* successful communication; there is no successful *entertainment.*

As entertainers, we're in the business of communication. ✳ = ✳ represents the successful communication of the *literal* meaning of an idea. In music, the ideas we strive to communicate are also charged with an *emotional* meaning. The songs we sing combine music and words to deliver both the literal and emotional messages equally well. Without words, songs are merely melodies. Without music, songs are merely poems.

Early in the twentieth century, audience-oriented singing came to rely on recording and broadcast as integral elements of the communication process. Popular entertainers no longer were present "in person" to project a song's central idea through personality, facial expression, gesture, and theatrical effects. Songs delivered long distance had to sell themselves. The words had to instantly convey, not only literal meaning, but the emotional context as well.

Historically, electronic reproduction, whether recorded or broadcast, sounded somewhat artificial. (Our ears have grown to accept the artificial sound as a more or less accurate representation of the live sound even as contemporary technology has steadily closed the gap between the two.) There were problems besides the artificial sound. In the range of human voices, low pitches were "heard" by the microphone less well than high pitches. Vowel sounds tended to record well, while some consonant sounds were relatively muffled and did not record well. Other consonants tended to record with an unnatural exaggeration of volume and presence.

Fred Waring and his dynamic staff of technicians, arrangers, singers, and choral directors experimented for years to find solutions to these problems. Through recordings, radio and television broadcasts, and amplified live concert appearances, they developed a system that counteracted the inherent limitations of electronic reproduction, especially as it affects the perception of sung lyrics. Their solutions have become the "standard" sound of popular singing. Solo singers sound like this. Recording artists sound like this. Jingle singers sound like this. Professional popular vocal ensembles sound like this. The technique is called "Tone Syllables."

*"Without words, songs are merely melodies. Without music, songs are merely poems. Songs combine music and words to deliver both the literal and emotional message."*

## TONE SYLLABLES

Fred Waring's Tone Syllable technique is not a list of *rules* to be thoughtlessly applied without exception. Tone Syllables is, instead, a *philosophy* that says, "Emphasize the meaningful and the beautiful. De-emphasize the extraneous, harsh, and artificial. Develop a personal interpretation of a song that will lead to an accurate and meaningful perception by the individual listener of the literal and emotional content of the song." Mr. Waring said, simply, "Sing all the beauty of all the sounds of all the syllables of all the words, and interpret accordingly." He felt that, for an American choir singing American songs to an American audience, the clearest *meaning* of the song grew out of the words, and the clearest *emotions* grew out of the sounds of the words.

> *"Sing all the beauty of all the sounds of all the syllables of all the words, and interpret accordingly."*

In a prose paragraph, certain sentences carry information that is most crucial to the delivery of an idea. Other, less important, sentences merely support, explain, or clarify the main idea. It takes lots of prose to get an idea across. Poetry, on the other hand, makes use of streamlined expression of ideas. Extraneous sentences and words are omitted. Poetry is simply more concise than prose. Poetry is the language of singing entertainers. Only essential words are used to convey an idea. Ideally, the communication is much more direct. The listener isn't expected to sort through superfluous sentences and words in order to uncover the central idea of the lyric.

Look at lyrics from an audience-oriented point of view. Which words absolutely *must* be perceived in order for the idea to get across? Which words, even in poetry, are there simply to make grammatical connections? Which words are most colorful and therefore elicit an emotional response? In any lyric, some words are more or less important in conveying the *literal* meaning; some words are more or less important in conveying the *emotional* meaning.

> "Given this explanation, don't you agree with me in many cases?"
> "Don't you agree with me?"
> "Agree with me?"
> "Agree?"

Some words important. Some not. Meaning still clear.

As a matter of fact, even each individual sound of a word may be more or less important or beautiful in conveying meaning and emotion. Consider the word LULLABY. Will you agree that the L sounds are *important* in understanding the word when it is spoken or sung? (Try saying the word without the L's!) On the other hand, say or sing the word LULLABY, but mess around with the UH vowel. Make it longer or shorter; modify it toward AH or IH or OO. You'll find that, as long as the L's are clear, the literal meaning of the word is pretty well understood. (By the way, in the word LULLABY, the soothing sound of the L's also expresses the emotional idea of the word.)

## ONOMATOPOEIA

Do you remember this term from your Sophomore English course? Onomatopoeia is the term for words that sound like what they describe. Pop! Whoosh! Zip! Pow! Now you remember; comic books are full of onomatopoeia. I think we, as interpreters, need to expand the number of words that fall within the definition of onomatopoeia. Lots of words sound like what they describe, but the correlation isn't as direct as in the comics.

Sing to yourself the first line of the old spiritual "There Is a Balm in Gilead." You used to think the word was "bomb" and wondered what it meant. Now, you know the word is "balm" and that it means some sort of soothing ointment you rub on a sore spot. Why did one of your Neanderthal ancestors, stooping by an oozing swamp to rub warm mud on a scrape, decide to name it "balm?" Stoop down. Rub the back of your hand gently. How does it feel? *(Don't say, "extraordinary", we haven't come that far in developing language, yet!)* Go find a pre-language baby. Rub something soothing on the baby. How does it feel? What "name" does the baby give the feeling? "Mmmmm." *Genius* baby has just invented onomatopoeia! The word sounds like what it describes: "Mmmmm." "Lllmmmm." "Ahallmmm." "Bahllmm." "Balm."

It probably took a few million years, but eventually the feeling, the action named "Mmmm", became "balm." Knowing that, how can you possibly, ever again, sing "There is a *balm* in Gilead" without coloring the AH to spell relief? How can you avoid lingering over the soothing LL and MMM? The caveman who lives in your brain will speak directly to the caveman who lives in my brain; we both remember "Mmmmm." "There is a *balm* in Gilead!"

> *"The caveman who lives in your brain will speak directly to the caveman who lives in my brain."*

Now take onomatopoeia one step further. Consider the sound of the word "Gilead". Say it a few times. Feel the primary accent on the first syllable: GIL-e-ad. Feel the weight rise off of the second syllable, and even more off of the last syllable: GIL-e-ad. Almost floats up out of your mouth, doesn't it?

Here is a picture of the accents of the word Gilead: a fifty-gallon drum full to the brim with cool, deep, still, motionless water. Here is a plastic beach-ball inflated to within a millimeter of bursting. Gently set the ball down on top of the water. Now, firmly press the ball into the water. Feel the resistance. Now, slowly relieve the pressure on the ball. (Don't let go suddenly ! Feel the ball rocket into the air if you let go suddenly? Let go *gradually*!) Feel it rise up against your hands. Say "Gilead". Press the ball into the water for the accent, and gently release if for the "unaccents": GIL-e-*ad*.

# Communication and Interpretation

"Gilead" is a very *vertical* word. Just like a palm tree springing up beside a pool of water in a desert oasis. Is that onomatopoeia? Does the word sound like what it is describing? Gilead. I think so. At least my cave-man right-brain thinks so. My choir thinks so.

## AMERICAN ENGLISH

Each language has its own characteristic sound. Imagine that you are suddenly swept up and magically transported to an unfamiliar foreign spot. Where are you? Listen to the babble of voices around you. Even if you don't understand a single word, can't you recognize the *sound* of the language? Is it French? What is the characteristic sound of French? Listen for inflection, tempo, pitch level. Your ear may not tell you the difference between German and Dutch or between Japanese and Chinese, but you'll agree there are great differences between sort-of-Germanic and sort-of-Oriental. Are you hearing sort-of-Scandinavian? Sort-of-Spanish? What is the characteristic sound of each of these?

> *"What is the characteristic sound of our language? What are the aural cues our brains easily decode?"*

Some languages come at you a mile a minute, while some others drawl out endlessly. Some are high pitched, some are gutteral, and some wander up and down the scale like a roller coaster. Some languages are accented at regular intervals, some ac-cent ev-er-y syl-la-ble, and some have an unpredictable pattern of accents. Some make use of rising inflection at the end of every word, some use glottal stops in the middle of words, some use exploded consonants, some use imploded or stopped consonants. The reason we have to work hard at understanding foreign accented American English is that the aural cues we are used to hearing are garbled with unfamiliar sounds and patterns. The sounds we aren't used to hearing, that need extra sorting out in our brains, are called "Noise."

Now imagine that a bewildered foreigner, dressed in his pajamas, magically appears in the middle of the local shopping mall. How will he know he is hearing sort-of-English? What is the characteristic sound of our language? What are the aural cues that our American-English brains easily decode? As an audience-oriented, perception-oriented entertainer, you need to be aware of these aural cues. You want the literal message to come through in a natural, non-artificial way. No "Noise." You want the emotional message to be just as direct. No "Noise."

Beware: *production*-oriented singing often calls for equal concentration and emphasis on every syllable of every word. In the search for uniformly "correct" vocal production, vowels are altered and consonants are exaggerated, sometimes beyond recognition. The result may well be "every beautiful pear-shaped tone", but it may also be unintentional "Noise". Your American audience isn't used to decoding five pure vowels and artificially emphasized final consonants. Their brains will have to sort through unfamiliar accents in order to perceive the message. Like the ladies on the streetcar, ✳ may eventually equal ✳ , but the extra work involved is not *perception-oriented*.

Also, don't be confused by the visual cues which serve to clarify meaning in written language. Written symbols are different from spoken or sung symbols.

> For a moment, try reading these words aloud one at a time, as though the visual spaces were meant to be aural cues.

Sounds unnatural, doesn't it? It will sound more natural if your run some words and phrases together: thesewords, oneatatime, thespacesweremeant. Now it *looks* unnatural, but it *sounds* natural.

Visual and aural cues are not the same. The visual cues include: *spaces, punctuation marks, upper and lower case letters, underlines, and italics.* The visual cues do not automatically correspond to the aural cues. Here are the aural cues we use to clarify meaning in spoken or sung American English: *volume and intensity* (loud or soft), *pitch* (high or low), *inflection* (rising or falling), *tempo and duration* (short or long), and *silence.* The composer makes some choices, the interpreter makes others. By manipulating the production of these elements we can insure accurate perception of the ideas our words and sentences represent— *successful communication!*

American singers entertaining American audiences with American songs should sing American English. The characteristic sound of our language includes: 1) a dramatic ebb and flow of accented and unaccented syllables, and 2) an infinitely broad palette of vowel and consonant colors. We call this "natural" enunciation.

For instance, as you read this paragraph *aloud* (pretend you are reading and explaining it to someone else), focus your concentration on the pitch and volume of the *accented* syllables. Of course there will be quite a variation, but you will soon be aware of a certain level of pitch and a certain level of volume that is your "peak" accent. (Try reading *this* sentence with every syllable at the "peak" pitch and volume.) Continue reading in your regular pattern. Now, focus your concentration on the pitch and volume of the *unaccented* syllables. Again, there is some variation, but you will notice that many of the connecting words and short, secondary syllables of words are almost mumbled. (Try reading *this* sentence with every syllable at the "low" pitch and volume.)

*"American singers entertaining American audiences with American songs should sing American English."*

# Communication and Interpretation

Both the all-accented and the all-unaccented interpretations sound false, don't they? Do you see the danger in production-oriented, "every pear-shaped tone" interpretation? It really contains just as much "Noise" as the lazy-tongue, lock-jaw syndrome we fight in untrained singers! The mistake that *trained* singers make in singing American English is seldom that we *over-accent* the *accented* syllables; it is, rather, that we tend to over-accent the *unaccented* syllables. Read that again: we tend to over-accent the un-accented syllables. You needn't sing any downright ugly sounds, but your singing will sound more natural if you are willing to make use of "un-accents!"

Both production-oriented singing and perception-oriented singing do have a number of elements in common: 1) breath control, 2) abdominal support of energized singing, 3) accurate phonation, 4) consistent resonance, and 5) clarity of tone. The major differences seem to lie in the realm of diction.

## POP DICTION

Remember the problems with recorded, amplified, and broadcast sound? Some sounds are easily "heard" by microphones, while others are nearly inaudible, and still others sound like sudden explosions. The standard diction techniques used in popular music were developed to counteract these early limitations. Today's technology has overcome some of the problems, but the basic techniques remain:

1) Sing a broad palette of "indigenous" vowels and diphthongs. American English has no limited number of pure, standard vowels.

> Of course all the vowels should be consistent in tone color within a song, but, for instance, the vowel UH in the word LOVE is natural, therefore correct, therefore beautiful. To modify it too far toward AH may make a more beautiful vocal sound, but may lessen the *emotional* meaning of the word. Of course, UH can be a very ugly sound if you sing it with poor tone color and no vibrato, but there is nothing inherent in UH that makes it less beautiful than AH. Sing the best UH and IH and EH you can, without apology. They are honest, sincere, meaningful sounds of American English.

2) Be aware of, and give consideration to, the unaccented portion of a diphthong or triphthong.

> The word BLOW isn't fully descriptive if only the pure OH is sung. In order to paint an aural picture of "air moving across the landscape," the audience must hear the word end in OO. Again, BLOH can be a beautiful sound, but BLOH+oo is more

*"Sing a broad palette of 'indigenous' vowels and diphthongs. American English has no limited number of pure, standard vowels."*

*meaningful.* (The problem of writing-out the sounds has always been problematic. Tone Syllables *look* ridiculous on the printed page; so do symbols of the IPA. It is better to understand that the techniques are an outgrowth of an underlying *aural* concept that can, only inadequately, be represented by any sort of *visual* symbols.)

Further, the unaccented portion of a diphthong or triphthong can be given a particular mathematical fraction of the duration of a word. This rhythmic subdivision based on word sounds lends an incredible vitality, drive, and clarity to the underlying rhythmic pulse of an up-tempo song, and a heightened sense of rubato and volume variation in a ballad. Look for words that are triplets or equally accented duplets (is there such a word?) or any other of the poetic "feet". String them together to create sentences that trip off your tongue and delight your inner sense of rhythm and meter. That's just what the poet or lyricist did. Discover (un-cover) the complex, ever-changing rhythm he has hidden within the basic pulse!

*"Rhythmic subdivision based on word sounds lends an incredible vitality, drive and clarity to the underlying rhythmic pulse."*

The *unaccented* portion of a diphthong may be *last* ("EYE" = AH + ee), or *first* ("YOU" = ee + OO). Often, this initial unaccented vowel will *precede* the beat and the main accented vowel will open *on the beat.*

Those "mystery vowels" from your childhood ("and sometimes Y and W") are often *heard* between words even though they aren't represented by a visual symbol ("YOU ARE" = eeOOwwAHr, which has a different aural effect from the "pure" but dry eeOOAHr). The hidden Y or W can be used to accent a word without the danger of a harsh glottal attack ("LIE OVER" = LAHeeYOHver, rather than LAHee:OHver).

Consider R to be a vowel which, like all the other vowels, may have a variety of tone colors. (Instead of thinking of it as 'that ugly consonant!') The word OUR becomes a triphthong (AHoorr) with a lovely strong vowel and two lovely fading vowels, rather than a misbegotten vowel that is bastardized by a couple of ugly consonants (AAwRR)! The vowel R is also, like Y and W, useful in avoiding a glottal accent ("FOREVER" = fohREHver, instead of fohr:EHver.)

3) Be aware of the consonant sounds (different from consonant *letters*) that are capable of sustaining pitch.

Some are relatively unpleasant: V, ZH, TH, while others are really beautiful: M, N; even L and NG. Because these consonant sounds drastically reduce the volume and audibility of the voice, give them added energy and duration. The listener will then perceive that the sounds to which you've added length and volume simply *match* the surrounding sounds.

These "tuned" consonants may be given a particular mathematical proportion of the length of a word. (As with the diphthongs and triphthongs, this proportion will probably be *felt* rather than arrived at by actual calculation!) Because of its added duration, an initial tuned consonant will generally *precede* the downbeat, and the main vowel will open *on* the beat ("AMERICA" = uhmmEHrihkuh, rather than uhMMEHrikuh).

(Jazz instrumentalists play "around the beat" as a matter of course. The pulse or "groove" remains constant, but attacks and releases don't have to happen exactly *on* the beats. Tasteful use of tuned consonants and diphthongs allows the solo singer and the vocal ensemble to *sing* "around the beat" by controlling when the main vowel of a given syllable begins or ends.)

4) In legato singing, don't let exaggerated consonants interrupt the smooth flow of vowel sounds unless they are needed to clarify the meaning of the text.

> *"Don't let exaggerated consonants interrupt the smooth flow of vowel sounds unless they are needed to clarify meaning."*

The French naturally "elide" the final consonant of a word to the initial vowel of the next word. When spoken, *"Beaux Arts"* has a Z in the middle of it. So does *"Champs Elysee"*. We do the same thing in spoken American English, but we don't make a big deal of it. When we say or sing "Night is over" it sounds more like "Nightisover." The sound of T becomes the *first* sound of a syllable and the sound of Z becomes the *first* sound of the next syllable. (The *written* symbols T and S *end* syllables, but remember that visual symbols and aural symbols are not the same!)

Whenever it enhances the legato line, without clouding the literal or emotional meaning of the phrase, let the last sound of a syllable become the first sound of the next syllable. Let sustained vowels and diphthongs carry the beauty of the tone.

5) In rhythmic singing, exploit the consonants that momentarily stop the flow of vowel sounds, both at the ends and in the middle of words.

Say "It could stop now." The tip of your tongue flips up to stop the vowels in the first two words; in the third word, your lips slam shut to stop the vowel flow. When you say an *isolated* T or D or P (or any other isolated "plosive" consonant), you start with tongue, teeth, or lips in place as an obstruction, then blow them out of the way with a puff of air.

Again, say "It could stop now." Chances are, that in the context of a sentence, you *don't* explode T or D or P. Once the consonants have done their jobs (momentarily interrupting the vowel sound), you probably slide your tongue, teeth, and lips around to get ready to make the next consonant sound— K or S or N— *without* an extra puff of air. This is the natural sound of American English. Remember, listeners "decode" aural cues in *groups*, *not* sound-by-sound (and *never* letter-by-letter; your ears have no interest in visual symbols!)

Say, "Let time...". You *see* two T's. Does your tongue wag up and down in order to expel two puffs of air? Ifuh ituh doesuh— "letuh timeuh"—thatuh soundsuh likeuh a foreignuh accentuh: "Let[uh]time." *Noiseuh!!* (Foreign accent: Do you say ak[uh]sent' or 'ak[stop]sent'?) Don't try to say *letters*; say *sounds*. Don't try to say *every* sound; sometimes it is silence that defines the "edge" of another sound!

Say, "And we're rockin' the Paradise." You have already learned to use the sound of D to accent "dwere" and you won't try to double-articulate the two R's: "we<u>R</u>ockin" is plenty. At a slow tempo, you will find the stopped k in the middle of "rok[stop]kin". Now, discover the stopped P between 'thP[stop]Paradise.' (Don't make too much of the vowel in the word "the". The word "the" is seldom accented in the context of a sentence. In "Rockin' the Paradise", it is reduced almost to 'thp'. The obviously *un*-pear-shaped vowel sound is only a momentary leak between two consonant sounds, TH and P.) The instant of silence before exploding "Paradise" gives energy, excitement, rhythmic drive, and *clarity of meaning*.

The clue to articulating "stopped" consonants is that the interruption of the vowel must be vigorous and, in a choral ensemble, exactly together. The teeth, tongue and lips may "slide around" a lot while going about the business of articulation, but they really have to *commit* to the job at hand when it comes to stopped consonants!

6) De-emphasize the sibilant sounds of S and SH.

Our ears hear the high-frequency sound of S better than any other vocal sound. So do microphones. Therefore, every S SoundS louder than the SoundS that Surround it. We're Seldom aware of it in Speech, but in Singing, the hiSSed S Syndrome is(z) the pitS!

> *"Exploit the consonants that momentarily stop the flow of vowel sounds."*

It is nearly impossible to suddenly take away vocal energy at the instant an S is sung. The Tone Syllable solution to the problem is to take the energy away from any vowel that precedes an S. If you're not pumping energy (therefore volume) through a vowel, you won't pump energy through the S that follows it.

Attack the vowel with normal volume, but quickly decrescendo in the moment before the S is sounded. It needn't sound false. It isn't a gimmick that is meant to draw attention to itself.

*"Quickly decrescendo the vowel before the S is sounded. It isn't a gimmick meant to draw attention to itself."*

In fact, none of the Tone Syllable techniques are meant to be evident. Think of them like Dolby noise reduction in recording. When listening to a Dolby recording, you aren't aware of how very silent the silences are; you probably aren't even aware that "Noise" is missing. The same is true of the diction techniques used in popular music. You aren't aware of the techniques; you just hear the words and sense the emotions without the "Noise."

Finally, these aren't *rules*. They are *concepts*. Sometimes you'll want to hiss an S for effect. Sometimes you'll need to double-articulate a consonant for clarity. Sometimes you'll be forced to twist a vowel out of shape or straighten out a diphthong for the sake of tuning or timing or drama. But, hopefully, you'll always want your American audience to hear *their* songs beautifully sung in *their* language. Here are the tools. Use them to build your own interpretations of American popular songs.

# 11. STAGING

## BALANCE

Consider *visual* balance on stage: numbers of people, height and weight, hair color, costume color, strength or weakness as a dancer. Also consider *psychological* balance. For example, the relative importance of a *soloist* on stage-right will balance a *group* on stage-left. The immediate visual imbalance is offset by the psychological balance. Similarly, the conductor need not always stand down-center with the choir symmetrically arranged up-center. For variety, move the conductor to one side and move the choir a little to the other side of center. The relative importance of the conductor will "balance" the stage.

In small groups on stage, girls should always stand in front of boys. Couples: *her* shoulder against *his* armpit; this closes the physical, and resulting psychological, space between them. The audience will perceive the couple (or a trio, or quartet) as a *single unit* on stage. In the case of two girls or two boys, short stands in front of tall. Be aware that positioning an "extra-tall" person even six inches further up-stage from everyone else will visually shorten him dramatically. (By the way, if you are blessed with a real odd couple— tall boy/short girl, or tall girl/short boy— pair them up as soon as possible in a little light-hearted bit, then try to avoid putting them together during the rest of the show. (see GLARING PROBLEMS, p. 122)

## CHIVALRY

On stage, in sight of the audience, boys should always move risers, microphones, props. Girls should not, unless, of course, it is somehow visually *less* gracious (hard to imagine), or destroys a traffic pattern, or is otherwise impractical.

## CHORALOGRAPHY

This term has come to be associated with esoteric movements that are designed to accompany Avant Garde choral works. I think it is useful to expand the definition. Consider every possible movement that can be executed with feet stationary. Stand in front of your full-length mirror. Isolate your head— up, down, left, right. Isolate shoulders, one arm, one hand, both arms and hands. Now turn to face stage-left or stage-right (leave your face— the source of vocal sound— toward the audience) and discover a whole new look for each of these moves and the nearly endless combinations. The value of CHORALOGRAPHY is that you can add visual interest in the tightest quarters and

*"You can add visual interest in the tightest quarters and with any number of performers."*

with any number of performers. Experiment with moves that define only vertical lines or only horizontal lines or diagonals. Everyone in the group need not do the same moves— work high in the back rows, low in front, and laterally on the edges.

### CURTSY

Girls should bow, not curtsy. The only exceptions include:
1) after a dramatic show-stopper in the classical vein, but only when wearing a long gown
2) a quick little Shirley Temple bob after a cute up-tempo solo
3) for comic effect, the "Prima Donna Squat" in which you slowly collapse clear to the floor, sit on your back foot, and kiss your front foot— the famous Dying Swan in ballet
4) always curtsy to the Queen of England

*"You slowly collapse clear to the floor, sit on your back foot, and kiss your front foot."*

### DEADPAN

Another comic effect, particularly for a "Country Cousins" family portrait. *No expression* is not enough. To read as comedy, we must see the EFFORT required to hold the freeze. (Think of the *long* time it takes the pioneer photographer to expose this frozen image on the old glass-plate negative.) Eyes wide, staring, and unfocused. Eyebrows high. Chin juts out. Extreme exaggeration of mouth movements.

### DUKE'S SEAT

Think about this: a symmetrical picture on stage can be perfectly "in-line" from only *one* spot in the house. It is the proverbial Best Seat In The House, dead center about two-thirds of the way toward the back of the house. For visual continuity and focus, the director should stage everything from this "ideal" vantage point. Each individual in the audience unconsciously adjusts his perception in relation to the DUKE'S SEAT. The director, watching and listening to rehearsals from this position, gives the entertainers a point to which they should project their performance.

### ENSEMBLE DISCIPLINE

Avoid every selfish movement. Even though *you* stood perfectly still and only scratched your ear *one time* during a song, the audience sees your group as a single entity which is constantly in motion... *You* just scratched your ear, then *he* just adjusted his glasses, then *she* just brushed her hair off her face, then *they* just glanced at the door opening in the back of the house, then *she* just scratched *her* ear, then *he* just smoothed *his* tie, then *she* just hiked up *her* slip... Pretty soon the audience gets the heebie-jeebies and runs screaming from the theatre! Not *your* fault. EVERYONE'S FAULT. Yours, his, hers, theirs! The drip of sweat on the end of your nose, the wisp of hair across your forehead, the wrinkle in your vest; each of these is *less distracting* when left alone.

## FIND THE LIGHT

Singers should be trained to find the "hot-spot"— the center area of maximum focus— in a pre-set spotlight. Too often we see amateur performers who "miss their mark" by a few inches, then end up standing with a shoulder and bow tie in bright light and their face in the dim, unfocused edge of the light.

## FOCUS

Whether or not there is a follow-spot to direct the attention of the audience, group focus should be *planned, rehearsed,* and *unanimous.* When the conductor is on stage, every eye must be there; each member of the audience will feel the intense interaction between conductor and ensemble and accept it as being directed at them personally.

Never glance away to see if the fly landed on Betty's nose, too. The sudden flash of the whites of your eyes distracts attention and makes the audience think maybe there is something *more* interesting than your show someplace else. Don't remind them!

During a down-stage featured solo, the focus of the ensemble and conductor should be on the soloist until a moment before the ensemble enters as accompaniment. To the soloist: *do focus your eyes.* So much has been said about looking at the back wall, or just above the heads of the audience. For heaven's sake, *include the audience in your focus!* We want to see in your eyes the changing ideas and emotions of your song as they register in your brain. At the end of a solo, be sure to "throw" the focus to the next person or area of action. Hold that focus for just an instant before you go on about your business.

Beginners are either catatonic or change focus and gestures too often...Really *look* wherever you've chosen to focus and *hold* for three or four seconds (it will feel like a long, long time!), then *change* your focus (with strength— don't let your eyes glaze, don't let your head bob around), and *hold* the new focus for another three or four seconds. As your message becomes more and more intense, hold each focus longer. In your mind, give each "photographer" in the audience (everyone) time to *see, check* the light meter, and then *capture* each focus, pose, or gesture.

*"The drip of sweat on the end of your nose, the wisp of hair across your forehead, the wrinkle in your vest; each of these is less distracting when left alone."*

# Staging

## FORMATIONS

Your basic college-choir-three-rows-of-choir-robes-or-tuxe-dos-just-stand-and-sing gets boring, even if the music is beautiful. Use a few basic visual contrasts to break the monotony. Try an "A-position" (bowling pins), a "V-position" (flying wedge), something with girls in the middle (in a contrasting costume), or boys in the middle. Experiment with symmetrical positions that dissolve during a key change into asymmetrical positions.

We're all used to a "two-choir" position that physically underlines the character of an antiphonal work— all you have to do is be a *little* more adventurous than that! *Rehearse smooth transitions* and traffic patterns from one formation to the next.

*This must be a lonesome sounding solo. At first glance, an asymmetrical formation, but the relative importance of the soloist, and his downstage position, psychologically "balances" the stage picture.*

*Here the soloist is at the same mic, but strong focus and proximity draw him into the group. Notice that it takes a quartet on stage right to balance the strength of the soloist.*

## GESTURES

Even "spontaneous" physical movement must be planned and rehearsed. Gestures need to be *appropriate* to the mood of the music and the meaning of the text. Gestures must look *purposeful*— feel a resisting force against the direction of your movement, and pose at the peak of the movement long enough for the audience to see that your gesture is *meaningful.*

Every gesture must return to neutral with *controlled* relaxation, and your hand and arm mustn't bounce or wobble once it is back in place. Take your time with each gesture. Know *why* it is happening, and don't make too many! One or two well-placed gestures are much more powerful than the ev-er-y-syl-la-ble-has-a-move-ment, "Stationary Dance Routine." Find a different outlet for your nervous energy.

## HOLD, BOW and GO

At the end of a solo, the singer must signal the audience to begin applauding by releasing the final gesture and focus, or looking up from a bowed-head, or with a grin and a tip of the head. *Then* the soloist takes one step to the side of the microphone (or a little step up-stage) and acknowledges the applause with a sincere facial expression, and *then* an appropriate bow. DO ONE THING AT A TIME! *Then*, one last look that says, "Thanks so much and I sure hate to leave." *Finally*, take one more step up-stage, still facing the audience, then turn away and back to position. Remember to "throw" the focus to the next point of interest.

## INCIDENTAL SOLO

Haven't you been distracted by inappropriate applause for a brief incidental solo in the middle of an otherwise *ensemble* feature? I think it is an outgrowth of the custom of applauding jazz players after *featured*, improvised solos. To discourage this, have the soloist stay in position at the microphone for several bars into the following phrase, *then* turn and gracefully rejoin the group. The effect will be enhanced if the soloist can give no indication of being anxious or uncertain when to "get back in line." At the *end* of the number, the incidental soloists can be acknowledged by a gesture from the conductor or a word by the Master of Ceremonies.

*"Pose at the peak of the movement long enough for the audience to see that your gesture is meaningful."*

### INDIVIDUAL BOW

*"A bow means 'I trust you not to poke me with your sword while I'm looking down.'"*

A bow should continue the mood and character of the song just ended. Don't end your inspirational or dramatic aria with an "aw gee whiz" nod of the head. Nor should you end an up-tempo rah-rah with the Ancient Cellist's creaky slow stoop!

Always keep your feet together throughout a bow. (Yes, even if you're really bow-legged!) Always *bow* your head— relax the back of your neck— look at your toes— show the top of your head to the audience— a bow means "I trust you not to poke me with your sword while I'm looking down." Don't try to keep eye contact with the audience. ("Which of you will hiss or throw old vegetables?") Hands relax at your sides and drop forward a little as you bow, then return to your sides as you straighten up. Use your face and eyes to express gratitude as you begin and end the bow.

### SIGN LANGUAGE

The use of American Sign Language has become widespread as a way to add visual interest to an otherwise static ballad. It *looks* beautiful to the audience, and *feels* even better to the performers! Inspirational, religious, and love songs seem to be naturally suited to this added interpretation. Signing can also be used to enhance the contrapuntal motion of a slow madrigal or to clarify a foreign language text.

In choral entertainment, sign language is used not for actual communication for the hearing impaired, but as aesthetic, artistic movement. In developing your sign language interpretation, look for the most poetic reading of certain words. For instance, "He ain't heavy, he's my brother." Does the text imply actual physical weight: *heavy*, or psychological weight: *bother, confusion,* or *trouble?* Certain signs are more pictorial, thus more visually poetic, than others.

Be aware of both the rhythmic character and the fluid character of signing. The little kid's action song, *"Don't be the boat if you can be the sail"* calls for small, bright, abrupt motions. *"You are so beautiful to me"* demands broad, legato movement. Again, look for, and exploit the varied vertical- or horizontal-ness that is inherent in many signs.

### SNEAK ATTACK

Simply: Don't reveal yourselves or your costumes or your show to the audience before the curtain rises!

## UPSTAGE

You UPSTAGE someone when, facing the audience, you stand slightly behind (up-stage of) them. Your position forces the other person to turn his back to the audience in order to face you directly. The term has come to mean anything visual or aural that draws attention to *you* at the expense of the other performers on stage.

## ZERO STANCE

Your neutral, do-nothing pose should be filled with vitality and energy. It is just like the stance for singing: a slightly aggressive lean toward the conductor or audience, one foot slightly forward, knees slightly flexed, chin up, shoulders back, not rigid, but with a feeling of suspension from the ceiling.

If you need to stand still for a long time (traditional choral concert), this stance allows you to shift your weight either forward or backward onto one foot or the other. Back-and-forth movement on stage is imperceptible (if you're slow and sneaky), while even the slightest side-to-side movement is a distraction.

Those standing on stage-left, put your *left* foot forward. Those on the right, *right* foot forward. This rounds everyone's shoulders ever-so-slightly to the center of the stage. At a microphone, or in a small group, your feet match your left-ness or right-ness in the group.

Feminine modification of the zero stance: Narrow the foot position to create a sort of one-point base. Soften the line of your arms by relaxing the elbows. You should have a general feeling of *lift* away from the floor. For power, masculine stance and gestures can look good on girls.

Masculine modifications: Wider foot position (at least shoulder width) to create a strong two-point base. Increase angularity of the arms—the feeling of sticky underarm deodorant—and a slightly more severe angle at the elbow. Fist position is stronger than relaxed fingers. Feeling of weight planted *into* the floor. For boys, feminine stance and gestures are seldom effective. (A softer look is appropriate, if well-controlled, in highly stylized jazz or 1940's era dance steps and poses.)

## STAGE AREAS

See page 97 for a diagram and explanation of the common labels for areas of the stage.

> *"Even your, neutral, do-nothing pose should be filled with vitality and energy."*

# 12. MIC TECHNIQUE

Much has been written about the kinds of equipment you should get and what-plugs-into-what. The technical considerations of a sound system are countless and, to me, complicated. My concern is that microphones and stands and cords and cables become a complement to, not a distraction from, *The Show.* Beginning actors learn to handle onstage props, furniture, and scenery thoughtlessly, with the same familiarity they treat objects in real life. Beginning entertainers should develop the same skills with microphones.

### APPROACH A MIC

Adjust the height of a mic stand *as* you step up to it. Don't first hit your mark, then correct your stance, and *then* reach out to fix the mic. Make the adjustment part of the overall approach before you get "settled."

The appropriate mic height for any situation except a rock concert is just slightly below your chin. Tip the mic up at about a forty-five degree angle toward your mouth. If you'll be at the mic for only a moment, you can make a minor adjustment by simply tilting it up or down a little. Otherwise, raise or lower the adjustable part of the stand with one hand while tightening with the other. *Never bend down* to try to speak "into" the mic; speak "across" it to your audience.

In any case, *rehearse* the adjustment until it becomes a smooth, automatic action that won't draw attention to the equipment and distract from you, the performer. If you will need to take the mic off the stand, know ahead of time what kind of clip attaches it and rehearse removing it and replacing it in one natural motion.

> *"Never bend down to try to speak 'into' the mic; speak 'across' it to your audience."*

*Simple rules of mic technique. First, don't hide your face. Second, as your survey the audience, move either your body or the mic to be sure it "hears" your voice!*

## BODY MICS

An expensive luxury for amateurs, a fact of life for professionals. The sensitive little microphone still has to be as close to your voice as possible and *you* have to be aware of twisting around so it is still between your mouth and your audience. The sound man has to be aware of, and control, the sudden volume boost that occurs when you and your leading man face each other for an argument or a love duet. You'll find countless uncomfortable ways to conceal the mic, the clip, the cord, the battery pack, and the antenna! You won't be the first to forget to switch your mic *off* as you rush offstage to the bathroom during rehearsal, and your technicians won't be the first to broadcast the local rock station, an ambulance call, or wedding during a performance!

> *"Your technicians won't be the first to broadcast a rock station, ambulance call, or wedding during a performance."*

## COUPLES

In a duet at a single mic, each performer sings to the two-thirds of the audience who are *across* the mic from them. The audience perceives the couple not as individuals, but as a single unit. Psychologically, the overlapping focus *does* reach out to the entire audience from the *unit.*

The singer on stage-right will necessarily need to "ignore" the people over his right shoulder, knowing that his partner is including them in *her* focus. Both singers should take advantage of non-singing moments— introduction, end of phrase, piano interlude— to include that off-mic audience in their focus. Turn away from the mic while you're singing and you destroy the music you've worked so hard to prepare.

### CROSS FOCUS

Again, whenever you sing or speak at a mic stand, always keep the microphone *between* your mouth and the audience's ear! Even a slight shift away from this CROSS FOCUS will lower your volume, and change the "presence" of your voice. When you look to your left, shift your weight onto your *right* foot to lean ever-so-slightly to the right. When you look right, lean left. Experiment with this technique until it becomes unselfconscious.

### FEEDBACK

Feedback is one of the things that draws unwanted attention to the sound system. Feedback is caused when the system starts to amplify its own amplification. Be sure to set up microphones up-stage of the speakers. If feedback starts, don't cup your hand over the mic; you just reinforce the cause. *Control* a hand-held mic even when you aren't singing. Don't accidentally point it toward speakers or monitors; you'll set up feedback. Feedback is one of the many reasons that your sound technician should be right there "monitoring" the system during rehearsals and performance.

A few other microphone do's and don'ts: Don't blow in a mic to test the system; the moisture in your breath is bad for the delicate insides. Don't thump on a mic; just say "Testing, one, two, three," or recite the Gettysburg Address. Don't try Rock Concert high-jinx with your microphones; rock stars can afford to throw mics around because they can afford to replace them!

### HAND HELD MIC

The reason for taking a microphone off the stand is to allow the singer freedom to move around the stage or into the audience. Too often, a microphone is taken off the stand just so an inexperienced performer will have something to do with both hands. One hand grips the mic and the other clutches at the cord. Soon nerves take over and the singer begins to "fiddle" with the cord in meaningless (and unconscious) gestures; she continually passes the mic from hand to hand; her mouth sings left, but her hand forgets and leaves the microphone to amplify her right ear! Use a hand mic for mobility, not as a visual crutch. It is much less distracting, and often stronger, simply to stand at a mic stand with your hands relaxed at your sides and let your face and voice sell the song.

*"Use a hand mic for mobility, not as a visual crutch."*

Like the stand mic, the hand-held mic should be just below your chin pointed toward your mouth at a forty-five degree angle. Press your elbow against your side and hold the mic *between* your mouth and the audience.

## LEAVE A MIC

Don't give 'em the cold shoulder!  After a solo at a downstage mic, back up two steps while still facing the audience.  Hold eye contact until the last moment, *then* turn toward center-stage to rejoin the group.  This allows you to break rapport *gently* and telegraph your exit before it actually happens.

## LOLLIPOP SYNDROME

Again, a catch-word to remind performers not to hide their faces with a hand-held or stand mic.  "If they can't see your face, you might just as well go home and phone it in!"  The technique of "eating the mic" is used by rock band singers in order to amplify the vocal sound over high volume instrumentals.  In that extreme situation, the technical concerns override the visual concerns.  In your solo or show choir situation, however, the instrumental volume shouldn't be that high, and the LOLLIPOP SYNDROME  is wrong.  (Exceptions, of course, for *purposeful* visual effect: a 50's Elvis look, or a T.V. gospel quartet.)

*"Learn to create an acoustical blend and balance that emphasizes the role of each individual."*

## MONITOR SPEAKERS

Monitors are useful for carrying accompaniment to far corners of the stage or for moving vocals closer to the band.  Monitors become a crutch when used to judge balance and blend *within* the singing group.

It is far more reliable to learn to create an acoustical blend and balance that emphasizes the role of each individual.  On-stage, each singer simply recreates his or her contribution *consistently*, even when it is "hard to hear" every other voice.  The unfortunate alternative is that every individual singer *and* the sound man are all constantly trying to adjust tone, volume, and pitch based on what they hear in the monitors. The magic ensemble sound never settles down and locks in.

## MOVE A MIC STAND

Keep one hand over the mic and clip (the thingie that holds it to the stand) and grab the bottom part of the stand with the other.  If you grab just the top half, it *will* come apart and you've left the base behind.  (Never happens in rehearsal, only in performance!)  Catch the cord with the hand that will hold the bottom part of the stand so that the tension of the cord is against your *hand* and not against the *plugs* at either end.  Remember the rule of chivalry on stage:  in nearly every situation, guys move the mics;  girls don't.

## PAGE

When using a hand-held mic, you need to keep the extra cord, not in a pile under your feet, but downstage in front of you. As you move down from an upstage position flip, "page", the cord forward and out of the way as part of your "choreography." *Rehearse!* As in dealing with the mics and stands, if your moves are *strong* and *purposeful*, the audience won't be distracted.

## PRESENCE

The term used to describe the sensation of intimacy or "proximity" to the audience's ear. Generally, think of the mic itself as the ear of each individual you sing to. The closer your mouth, the more intimate or commanding your message.

*Dealing with choreography, you must make conscious decisions concerning the constantly changing ratio of "importance" of movement versus sound.*

# 13. CHOREOGRAPHY

**ACTOR'S APPROACH**

Here is the approach to creative movement that you've been using since before you were in Kindergarten— ACT OUT THE SONG. The simplest level is to create an action for *each word* of a song. *"Three blind mice, three blind mice,"* —you remember: hold up three fingers on each hand, then fingers cover your eyes, then on top of your head to become little mouse ears. *"Three blind mice!"*

Much the same are movements that describe, not individual words, but *each phrase* of a song. *"The itsy bitsy spider climbed up the water spout,"* all together now: thumbs and fingers criss-cross laboriously into the air, the rain falls amid wiggling fingers, and the sun comes out in a burst of open palms. So far, this is very basic and even trite, but remember the Supremes made millions just like this, *"Stop, in the name of love, before you break my heart!"* At least it leads us to the next, more creative steps.

For example, *"I've been working on the railroad all the live-long day."* The song doesn't say exactly what work, so you create: pounding spikes, shoveling coal, riding one of those see-saw-powered handcars; or how about being the conductor who tips his hat then punches each ticket? You have become an "actor" who moves in character based on the *implied idea* of the song.

The final step is a song like *"In that great gettin' up mornin' fare ye well, fare ye well,"* that doesn't describe any action at all. Now, you must *invent* a scene in which movement is possible. Let's make it an old-fashioned Camp Meeting with a fire-and-brimstone preacher and a jubilee-revival-shout congregation. Create the basic picture on stage: either symmetrical (congregation lined up in "church pew" rows on both sides of the down-stage soloist), or asymmetrical (the focus is up-stage toward the preacher on the top step of the risers— various clusters of sinners must turn around abruptly to chant their chorus to the audience).

Now that you've created a basic picture, what movement— what "choreography"— will your congregation do? Start simple; what do *real* revival congregations do? Well, they sway side-to-side. Now, what *must* they do because they are on stage? Of course. They have to turn back over their shoulders to sing to the audience. Now let them get a little theatrical: they lean toward the preacher and reach out to him; they reach up toward heaven and shake their hands; they suddenly point directly at the audience to reinforce the Good News; they clap

> *"Here is the approach to creative movement that you've been using since before you were in kindergarten."*

# Choreography

rhythmically— quietly and close to the body, or loudly above their heads; one hand becomes a tambourine that slaps against wrist, elbow, or thigh, then shakes high in the air; now they stand up, sit down, and kneel. None of this action is expressed in the lyric, but each singer is an actor in a scene you have created from the general *idea* of the song!

*"How to make 'acting' in 'choreography'? Rhythm, Direction and Focus."*

How to make their "acting" into "choreography?" The answers are to be found even in our basic elementary school examples: RHYTHM, DIRECTION, and FOCUS.

Just as movements in "Three Blind Mice" happen on each beat, so, too, must the spike pounders and tambourine shakers execute their moves *rhythmically*. You'll choose to vary the underlying pulse to fit the character of your scene— eighth-note excitement or whole-note drudgery. Sometimes the action even freezes for a few counts, but it is all always rhythmic.

Second is *direction*. Your itsy bitsy spider "climbs" in a strong vertical action from your chest to high above your head. He is "washed out" in a diagonal movement that starts way above your head and swipes down and out as far as you can reach. Sometimes you'll want *unanimous* direction (everybody's right hand is a tambourine that goes up on beats one and three). Other times you'll look for as much *variety* as possible (one group shovels coal horizontally from left to right, while the handcar riders pump vertically from deep-squat to tippy-toes, and the spike pounders work diagonally from right to left). Every move has a strongly defined direction.

Finally, for the actor's approach to work, the face as well as the body must be involved. *Focus* on your spider as he crawls up and up; your head and eyes and even eyebrows follow the direction of your hands. The movement becomes defined and believable to the audience. Always use your face to reinforce the character and emotion of your acting!

## BARNUM and BAILEY

This is one of my personal terms coined to describe any sort of huge, three-ring-circus pose. You'll probably have a different name for the same idea, but the point is that whether you call a position a Clump, or Squash, or Amoeba, that you *do* give it your own colorful, descriptive, and memorable name. Of course there are certain standard terms for some things, but if your novice singer/dancers shy away from something called a "Demiplié," call it the Half-Squat!

## BLACK OUT

Leave a final pose illuminated for a beat or two to allow the picture to "burn-in" in the audience's eye before the stage goes dark. An *abrupt* blackout generates continued excitement and draws applause, while a mere *fast fade* to black encourages warm, rather than wild applause. Performers will learn to feel that momentary fade time when they must remain motionless even after the lights go out. There is a split second, before the audience is blinded, when they can be disappointed to see the freeze break.

## CHEERS

Some exciting moments seem to call for "spontaneous" whoops and screams and cheers from the singers. The trick to spontaneity is meticulous rehearsal! In most cases, work toward a variety of pitches and various durations of yells (well-supported from the abdomen with plenty of breath!). Assign a few voices to anticipate the cheer and a few to overlap into the next section, otherwise we hear: *"...red, white, and blue!"* SILENCE "hooRAAYYY" SILENCE *"three cheers for our..."*. The effect seems stilted and false.

It is never appropriate for performers to scream a "victory yell" after the final curtain falls— no matter how great the achievement. No matter how much hard work and anxiety has gone into a production, don't let the audience see the price tag! The same deportment and *controlled* energy that characterized the opening of your show should carry through until the audience is out of ear-shot.

> *"No matter how much hard work and anxiety has gone into a production, don't let the audience see the price tag."*

## CLAPPING

Here is another way to add rhythmic aural and visual excitement to a number. It is great to clap while you sing, but don't let enthusiasm drown out the vocals! Clap the heel of your hand for less volume, or pull-your-punch at the instant of contact.

*Rehearse* exactly when to start and when to stop. If the clapping is supposed to be spontaneous, *assign* who begins and who joins in. In our culture rhythmic emphasis is usually on beats 2 and 4. I guess maybe an Irish jig claps *on* the downbeat, but rock music doesn't and spirituals don't. Clapping on 1 and 3 seems like the final grand promenade of a slightly baggy Russian One-Bear-Only Circus. The point is, *decide* which is appropriate and why.

## COMPANY FRONT

The name given to that long single line, shoulder-to-shoulder, facing the audience across the front of the stage. Use a company

# Choreography

front in the last few bars or key change into a Big Ending, for a kick-line, a ripple bow, or a sudden sweep from up-stage down onto the apron before a blackout.

## DANCER'S APPROACH

One basic definition of "dance" is: "To move rhythmically to music using prescribed or improvised steps and gestures." The ACTOR'S APPROACH dealt mostly with gestures, and the DANCER'S APPROACH deals mostly with steps. In building choreography from either point of view, there may be moments to improvise— to "do your own thing"— but *mainly*, the movement will be prescribed, dictated by the choreographer.

Dance at its most basic exists for its own sake. It doesn't need to tell a story or convey a mood or even be beautiful. Simply move your body because it feels good! However, once we decide to use dance to enhance the presentation of a song, certain guidelines must come into play.

*"Dance is simply a succession of poses; if the poses match, the connecting movement will be uniform."*

Most important is that the movement not interfere with good vocal production, nor obscure the musical and poetic aspects of the song. (There *are* some exceptions; see PRODUCTION NUMBER, p. 95.) In fact, the movement ought to be harmonious with the rhythm, tempo, mood, and form of the *music*, and should complement the meaning and mood of the *text*. Dancers are generally sensitive to the aesthetic and musical aspects of a song, but often less sensitive to vocal and textual demands. Your job as PRODUCER/DIRECTOR gives you the *ultimate* responsibility for the success of the choreography. You need to guide your dancer/choreographer toward understanding these added "restrictions." "If you're throwing your head around in circles you can't sing. Anything else, let's give it a try!"

The difference between the Actor's and the Dancer's approach to movement has mostly to do with meaning. As I said, dance doesn't have to *mean* anything. The classical *Arabesque, Pas de bouree,* and *Pirouette* don't convey any particular meaning, but neither do the popular *Waltz, Charleston,* or *Twist,* nor the vaudeville *Grapevine* and *Shuffle Off to Buffalo.* No inherent meaning, yet each of these movements expresses a certain attitude and mood and has certain associations for a majority of your audience. They will work wonderfully to heighten the effect of the appropriate song. (Some dance steps *do* have an underlying idea. The *Pas de chat* represents a leaping cat, and the *Turkey Trot* is, well, like your great-grandmother doing the *Funky Chicken.*)

Consider dance not as a "series of motions," but rather, a "succession of poses." Even the simplest movement must have a starting point and an ending point— two frozen moments that define the "edges" of the movement. To my eye, *clean* choreography must have crisp edges. Your untrained dancers probably give great energy and precision to the movement part of a step, but are sloppy at the frozen edges. If the *poses* match, the *movements* that connect them will be uniform. Questions of how-high-the-hands, what-twist-the-shoulders, and where-exactly-the-left-heel become not "extra polish," but *essential* points from the beginning.

The elements of RHYTHM, DIRECTION and FOCUS are equally important in both the Actor's and the Dancer's approaches to choreography. Dance choreography, because it doesn't necessarily depend on the story of the song for its impetus, must also add FORM and GROWTH.

Some steps are more exciting than others, some are inherently legato or staccato, or more or less expressive in a given context. Be sure to construct your choreography to complement the purely musical aspects of your song! If there is a three-page crescendo to the end of a piece, your choreography should build in excitement through the same three pages.

Finally, various approaches to creative movement are not mutually exclusive. The same effect on stage can be reached whether you start at the barre, or start marching, or start as an actor! There is no "best" approach and there is no "best" result— the same song can have a thousand effective visual interpretations. The important thing is that the movement not be *arbitrarily imposed* without some underlying motivation. Meaningful choreography *grows out of* the performers; it makes sense to them and is appropriate to their abilities, experience, and temperament.

*"Even the simplest movement must have a starting point and an ending point— two frozen moments that define the edges."*

## ENSEMBLE BOW

A group bow may be worked into the choreography rhythmically, either in silence or underscored with "bow music." "*Pose*-two-three-four, *smile*-two-three-four, *break*-two-three-four, *down*-two, *up*-two, *hold*-two-three-four." Or the group may take a cue from a leader down-center. The leader needs to make only a *small* anticipatory movement. Head and shoulders rise slightly as if to take a quick breath. The tempo and character of the bow should match the song just ended, either elegant or vigorous.

A vigorous bow is executed as follows:

1) Feet together, lift your chin and chest as you rise slightly onto your toes— like beginning to dive into a swimming pool. At the same time, throw your wrists (hands relaxed) slightly forward (elbows bent slightly).

# Choreography

2) As the weight transfers back to your heels, let your arms pull your head and torso down— relax the back of your neck to look down at your toes. (Your hands continue a natural swing down and back to a point a little behind your legs.)
3) As your body bounces back up, your forearms swing forward again (but not so far as the original wrist-throw), pulling you up onto your toes again.
4) Arms settle back to a relaxed position as your weight transfers back to your heels.

(You should feel an inhalation to begin, and a slight hesitation at the peak of steps 1 and 3.) The audience must see your teeth and eyes sparkle as you drop forward, and again, as you bounce back up. Remember that the *purpose* of a bow is to say "thank you" for applause.

## ENTRANCE

Here is a project for the Wednesday morning following your Tuesday night concert, when nobody feels much like singing anyway. Experiment with setting up your risers in unusual ways, then try different ways of getting there from off-stage. Up over the back, down the center aisle, alternate rows from different directions, herd style, etc. The project doesn't have to be strictly disciplined, but you'll have several gimmicks ready to polish-up for the next show.

## EXIT

If you don't have a curtain, *organize your exit* over bow music. While most of the performers exit fast, choreograph a few various points of interesting action to hold the audience's attention until the last "bit" of business center stage or nearly-in-the-wings. One last wave, a dance step, or comic bit, and suddenly (it seems), the stage is empty.

*"If you kick high enough or long enough, the audience will applaud!"*

The common error is that after the last bow *everyone* turns to "exit stage-left" and we are left to watch 20 seconds of Ears and Rears leaving the stage! If the exit follows a company front bow, the last few people (one end or the other— or center, if you split to exit) continue to face the audience, holding their attention for two or three beats before turning to exit.

## KICK LINE

One of the oldest Vaudeville truths: "If you kick high enough or long enough, the audience *will* applaud!" The company-front, step-kick-step-kick can be overused, but it has become a cliché because it *works*.

Stay in control of the movement throughout. Work to match the height of the kick, even if it means lowering a few to match. An instant of freeze at the top of the extension adds crisp definition. Always point your toe. (To visually lengthen your leg, turn your toe *in* just slightly.)

## MAGNIFICATION

Every move you do is multiplied by the number of people in the group. A small sway in each body becomes a major left-to-right motion by the entire ensemble. A big sway that just looks energetic in each body can become uncontrolled and ridiculous in the big picture. Always be aware and willing to modify your planned choreography to fit the size of your group. The great idea you saw at a summer workshop may have looked terrific on ten people, but needs to be changed for your thirty-two. On the other hand, the clever little T.V. move for eighty or one hundred won't "read" when executed by your smaller group.

## POOF

Another silly name to describe a concept. Make up your own name if you like, but *use* the concept! In animated cartoons, the characters tend to leap into the air and pedal their legs for a second or two before actually making any progress. Live characters on stage need to create the same sort of tension and release each time they move from position to position. The feeling is of a little internal explosion that lifts your chin and shoulders and elbows— you could even rise a little onto your toes. Hold that suspension for an instant, then relax into the move to a new position. The POOF changes size and character as the mood of the music or pace of the transitions change, but it should always be present.

## PRODUCTION NUMBER

Sometimes the music moves you to a great idea that really pulls out all the stops. Every once in a while, choreography and special effects can take precedence over text and choral tone. There is nothing wrong with this, as long as you make a *conscious decision* to emphasize the secondary elements for one number. Don't let your show become all flash with little supporting musical integrity. Any production number will seem bigger, by contrast, if you surround it with less bombastic numbers.

## RIPPLE

A trick to make a simple move look more complicated than it really is. A dancer at the end of a row starts a given move (kick, bow,

> *"Don't let your show become all flash with little supporting musical integrity. Make a **conscious** decision to emphasize the secondary elements."*

turn, etc.) immediately followed by each successive person in turn. Precision drill teams have raised this effect to a high art— *precision* is the key. A ripple can also move from the center towards the ends, or start at both ends simultaneously, or happen, not in a line, but in a symmetrical or asymmetrical formation.

## STAGE DIRECTIONS

I'll bet you've been looking for this entry. Stage-right and stage-left relate to the right and left of the *performer on stage* facing the audience. Before someone invented the slanting theater floor, in which each row is seated slightly above the row in front of them, *stage* floors used to be built at an angle slanting toward the audience, so everyone could see. The position closest to the orchestra pit really was *down*-stage, and *up*-stage toward the scenery was an uphill climb!

Visually and psychologically, downstage positions are "stronger" than upstage. (You are bigger and closer— easier to see and easier to hear.) Because the audience reads left to right (stage-right to stage-left) the eye automatically looks to stage-right first. Thus, stage-right is stronger than stage-left. Down-center, where the conductor probably stands, is the strongest of all. (See STAGE AREAS p. 97.)

Just a few other things: microphones and light positions are usually numbered from stage-right to stage-left. The opening that lets the audience see into the stage area is called the *proscenium.* The stage floor in front of the proscenium is called the *apron. Wings* are the off-stage areas left and right. The area behind the back curtain is a *cross-over.*

*"Football teams learn the names of the white lines and the tall poles. Performers need to learn the names of their arena, too."*

Use theatrical terms when working and learning in a theater. "Football teams learn the names of the white lines and the tall poles. Performers need to learn the names of their arena, too."

## UNDERLYING PULSE

Some choreographers tend to build *every* number on the quarter-note pulse: "Ev-e-ry-syl-la-ble-has-a-move-ment-all-its-own-that-does-n't-stop-un-til-the-end-of-the-show." Some songs work great that way, but others need the variety of slower or faster rhythmic movement. And, just as harmonic movement can change in the middle of a number, so can the underlying choreography pulse. In every way, exploit opportunities for variety and the unexpected!

# STAGE AREAS

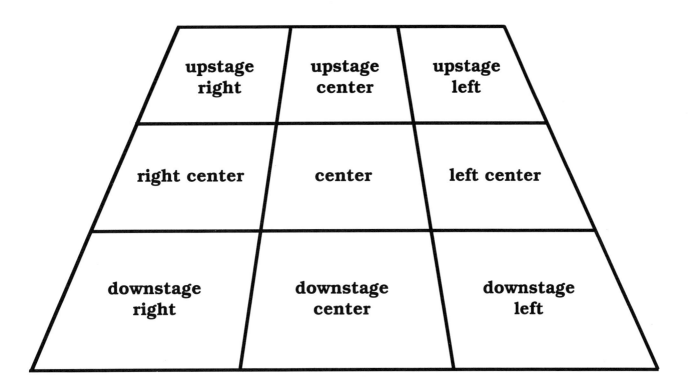

AUDIENCE

# 14. PROGRAMMING

## CONTRAST

Here is the best example of extreme contrast I've ever seen: Victor Borge and his featured soprano spent ten or fifteen minutes building an onstage argument from clever to caustic to furious (teasing the audience from smiles to belly-laughs). She suddenly threw her nose in the air and stomped off the stage. The audience literally screamed with laughter and poked their elbows in their neighbor's ribs and stamped their feet and cried!

Instantly, the piano was bathed in a pool of blue light. Mr. Borge sat perfectly still playing stately arpeggios as the laughter jerked fitfully to silence. From far-off in the wings we heard the disembodied, ethereal voice of the soprano singing the Gounod AVE MARIA. A profound stillness fell over that enormous audience as tears of mirth became tears of awe. We really heard that old "chestnut" with new ears!

I'm sure it would have been lovely if she had sung it onstage after a serious introduction, but the abrupt and unexpected emotional contrast heightened her solo to a moment of transcendental beauty. Look for opportunities to build *unexpected* contrasts into your programming.

*"A profound stillness fell over that enormous audience as tears of mirth became tears of awe."*

## CHESTNUT

A "Chestnut" is a song that has gone through every phase of popularity: hit, cliché, passé, and back around into the collective cultural memory. Everybody knows the tune and most of the words, but nobody quite remembers just who the composer was. When you go to a lecture, you like to hear at least a few things you already know. When you read a novel, you like to recognize some of the people and places and situations. Your prior knowledge helps you relate to the unfamiliar elements that are introduced. At your shows, your audience is just like you! Share a couple of the old favorites.

## ENCORE

Your encore can either *top* the finale, or it can be a dramatic *denouement* from the emotional high of the finale. The simplest encore is a brief reprise (pronounce ruh<u>preeze</u>, not <u>ree</u>prize) of the opener or an audience favorite from the middle of your show. Use an encore to show off the *best* feature of your group—the *last* impression is as important as the first. Sing your most beautiful choral sound as the curtain falls. (Unless everybody tap-dances better than they sing, then end with a dance feature!)

## FINALE

The finale should top everything that has come before it, both aurally and emotionally. This is the moment to pull out all the creative "stops." These are guaranteed audience-pleasers: patriotic, inspirational/religious, up-tempo, familiar, or emotional high. Little Miss Liberty with a paper-mache torch and a baggy-pants Uncle Sam in a cotton-ball beard have *always* worked in a one-room school house; the same sort of thing will work for you, no matter how sophisticated your audience.

## GEM

The name given to a song that is entirely different from everything around it— a feature, but more unusual. A GEM could be an a cappella work in an otherwise accompanied program, a solo feature set apart from the ensemble texture, a novelty contrast in a classical concert, or a classical work in the middle of a light program. (Someday, somebody will use Debussy's DIEU QU'IL LA FAIT BON REGARDER as the close harmony, a cappella ballad in a Show Choir Festival and stand the audience on their ear!) The advantage of the GEM concept is that some of your audience will be exposed to an out-of-context style of literature they might otherwise never hear.

## NOSTALGIA

Here's a good exercise to do every few years: Your students are between 13 and 18 years old. They are just now near the peak of establishing their life-long preference for a certain sort of "pop" music (whatever the current styles are). Their parents went through the same process when *they* were in school. Chances are, the parents of your students are your "primary" audience, so picture them as High School students and consider *their* favorites to be "songs of the good old days!" (It takes some figuring, since your student might be the oldest child of young parents or the baby of a long line, but you can narrow it down to a particular decade.)

## OPENER

The audience's perception of the character of your show will be set within the first minute. One minute! If it takes two minutes for three long lines of choir robes to file onto the risers, the emotional message you've established is one of repetition and delay. By the time

> *"Little Miss Liberty and Uncle Sam have always 'worked' in a one room school house. The same sort of thing will work for you."*

you start to sing, it'll be an uphill battle to regain audience interest. A solemn processional is sometimes appropriate, but it must be re- hearsed and timed so it doesn't become a pointless "slow-shuffle" without focus and direction.

For an up-tempo opener, look for what I call a "one-beat" song— a number in which the underlying beat is a brisk one, one, one, one, one, one... *"When you're down and out, lift up your head and shout..."* or *"Another op'nin' another show..."* or *"C'mon baby, let the good times roll..."*

A "two-beat" number— one with a breezy, swinging, strong/weak pat- tern— is a good *second* number, but not driving enough for an opener. (Other good second numbers: jazz waltz, up-tempo Latin, familiar up- tempo nostalgia or novelty.)

## PRE-SHOW

You might take advantage of the audience waiting in the lobby to establish the character of your show. A Circus theme would logically call for a juggler or magician to entertain (and control the flow of people into the house). The comedienne Lily Tomlin, dressed as a Red Cross nurse, served hot coffee to freezing people standing in the ticket line for her Broadway show! Poster-size photographs of rehearsals and per- formance, an elementary school art exhibit, and the brass quartet playing Christmas carols all come under the heading of pre-show. If your show is part of a dinner-theater concept, you might work up a little five-minute segment to "tease" the audience after they are seated, before the meal is served.

## SEASON

Your initial promotion for the year should focus, not just on the Fall Concert, but on your entire season: Fall Concert, Holiday Vespers, Variety Show, Music-in-Our-Schools Festival, Choir Tour, and Spring Home Concert. Your audience begins to establish loyalty to "macro- programming"— they'll be back for each event of the series.

## SOUP CAN

The directions on a can of Cream-of-Mushroom soup call for you to "gradually add one can of milk to the soup while heating to simmer." But, how many people add only *half* a can of milk? Who adds three- quarters of a can of *water*? Or dump the whole thing into a green bean casserole to take to the Methodist basement supper? Do you have any

*"You bought the music. Use it as an ingredient in creating your show."*

# Programming

reservations about being creative with the ingredients you've purchased?  The Soup Company has, in exchange for your money, relinquished proprietary rights in that can of soup to *you*, the consumer.

Look at a choral octavo in just the same way:  you bought the music, use it as an *ingredient* in creating your show.  The arranger didn't know that I wouldn't have tenors this year.  The publisher didn't know that I need just one verse and the key-change chorus to get from Position A to the down-stage blackout.  Mozart didn't know that we need just the Alleluia section after the spoken benediction.

As a producer, look on arrangers, composers, and publishers as sources for show-building *material*.  Certainly you must compensate them for their efforts, then *use* their contributions in whatever way is most effective for your unique situation. (See COPYRIGHT LAW p. 143). You can't re-sell the Mushroom Soup as your own, and you can't pass off a "doctored" arrangement as your own creation.  Musicologists hold an attitude of "sanctity" toward the great masterworks that we need not transfer to the material we use in building *The Show*.

*The printed score is only a starting place for your creativity in building a program.  Always bear in mind, though, that the music is always the heart of your show!*

# THE *Art* OF ENTERTAINMENT™

# III

# PRESENTING THE SHOW

*"Sincerely, Yours"*

# "Sincerely, Yours"

*TA DA!! IT'S FINISHED! Well, not quite.*

*Singer/dancer/friend Patsy Garrett (you know the "chow, chow, chow" lady on TV) used to remind us that anyone can give a present to another and in whatever way it's offered it will generally be appreciated. But, the same present, tastefully wrapped with lovely colored paper, tied together with a matching ribbon, and accompanied by a sensitive card is suddenly a "gift". Just as suddenly such a "gift" is much more fun to give and immeasurably more enjoyable to receive.*

*Your entertainment package is the present you offer to your audience. The fine music, the clever staging and classy costumes will all be generally appreciated if you've done your homework. The making of your offering into a "special gift" will depend now on how you "wrap it up." The attention to the final details will demonstrate the care you feel for your product and your audience. It will not go unnoticed. When people visit Walt Disney World they automatically "ooh" and "aah" over Cinderella's Castle, Space Mountain, and the Small World Dolls. That is not surprising. But often when the vacationers return home it is remarkable that what impressed them the most were not towering spires, a roller coaster ride or an electric light parade. It was instead the trash cans shaped like tree stumps in Frontierland, the stantions topped with gargoyles at the Haunted Mansion, or the way the butter pads are embossed with mouse ears at the Crystal Palace Restaurant. Attention to detail is what makes The Show a "special" gift.*

*The Show begins long before the orchestra plays the overture or the performers step onto the stage. Like the perfect gift, your best performances will be the ones that were given a lot of thought and an early, extra effort to make them special and "sincerely, yours!"*

> *"Like a perfect gift, your best performances will be the ones that were given a lot of thought and an early, extra effort to make them special."*

# 15. GROOMING

For anyone who dared to appear in public looking sloppy, my grandmother had a withering look and a disparaging remark: "It looks as if he was sent for and couldn't come." These GROOMING guidelines are based on a youthful, clean-cut, All-American look. Polish your shoes. Comb your hair. Check your costume for ravelings and your stockings for runs. Be sure your costume is clean and pressed. It is all just common sense, but questions will arise, so your performers should be aware of the attitudes of "the pros."

*"For anyone who dared to appear in public looking sloppy, my grandmother had a withering look and a disparaging remark: 'It looks as if he was sent for and couldn't come."*

## CONDUCTOR

Be especially aware that your face communicates to your choir. Keep your hair off your face. Give attention to grooming the *back* of your hair and to pressing the *back* of your costume— that's what the audience sees!

## FACIAL HAIR

A beard, moustache, or long sideburns creates a blurred look on most stage faces. A moustache, even when neatly trimmed, visually turns down the corners of your mouth and makes a shadow that hides the sparkle of your smile. If your moustache is one of those first-attempt-smudges and you won't shave, use an eyebrow pencil to fill in the blanks! Sideburns need to balance the shape of your haircut, but avoid anything that extends below the middle of your ear.

## FINGERNAILS

Guys: clean and trimmed. Girls: trimmed or shaped without exaggeration. Clear polish or neutral beige or brown enhances the clean-cut, Youth-of-America look. Your ensemble look would have to be really formal and sophisticated to justify deep, rich, red nail polish. Avoid *personal* extremes— purple, gold, orange— unless your whole show goes Punk!

## FOUNDATION GARMENTS

For some reason everyone laughs when the subject of appropriate underclothes is raised, but you'll need to impress on your performers— women and men— that your show is not a platform for a statement of personal liberation!

# Grooming

## HAIR

The length and grooming of your hair can add or detract from the overall image of the group. Because the shadow cast by any overhead lighting hides your eyes, keep your hair off your forehead. (Advisers to political candidates say at least 3/4 inch above the brow for men.) To accentuate an elegant, formal look, girls can pull their hair up and off the face to expose temples, ears, and the lovely silhouette of neck and shoulder. The clean-cut look for boys calls for the hair to just touch ears and collar. If your group is physically active on stage, everyone spray your hair with unscented hairspray. Again, personal extremes distract from the feeling and image of ensemble. No flowers, no beads, don't dye your hair blue, and don't have Aunt Aurelia's hairdresser create a beehive with a birdcage in it. Combs and barrettes should match your haircolor, not your costume.

## PERFUME

No. No. No. Lots of people experience a mild reaction to perfume, cologne, hairspray, and designer deodorant. Even a slight swelling of the membranes in your nose, mouth and throat will affect your vocal production. Take a bath before you go on stage, be sure your costume is clean, and use unscented deodorant. (This is not the time to experiment with some herbal concoction from the Whole Earth Catalog!)

*"Makeup is as much a part of your show as costumes and smiles."*

## MAKEUP

Entertainment is cosmetic. It is bigger and better than real life. Makeup is as much a part of your show as costumes and smiles. Women should wear makeup that will complement the formal or informal nature of their costumes and the overall image and character of your show. In natural light, for a small audience, it is often enough to simply brighten the eyes and highlight cheeks and lips a little. (Remember, the brighter the stage lights, and the bigger the room, the more your makeup will need emphasis.) Guys, in order to complement the girls, will need a little cheek color (think shades of brown, not red), and some eye brightening.

## WHITE SOCKS

Once an administrator called me into his office just before the first concert of the year. "Be sure to remind the boys not to wear white socks with their suits." Obviously! I almost laughed out loud until I realized he was serious and speaking from bitter personal experience. When *he* was in the school choir, no one thought to tell him not to wear white socks; instead, they laughed behind his back. *Embarrassment* was his most vivid memory of singing in the High School Choir. Don't take the details for granted. White socks go with white shoes and white trousers, not with dark slacks, and not with a suit.

*Use your energy as a performer first in your mouth (notes, words, tone quality); second in your face (sincere response to changing emotional message); and finally in your body (staging and choreography).*

# 16. TECHNICAL SUPPORT

### CALL BOARD

The one place in a theater where the "official" time, place, and date of each rehearsal is posted. Your classes probably meet on a daily or regular basis, but get in the habit of posting all other rehearsals, meetings, and performances just outside your rehearsal room or office.

The CALL BOARD accomplishes two things: it keeps each person up-to-date on the schedule he is committed to, and it creates a sense of urgency and continuing activity for everyone involved in your program.

### CURTAIN WARMERS

Stage lights do "animate" the colors and textures of the inanimate elements of your show— instruments, the set, props, costumes, and the curtain. If you are lucky enough to have stage lighting, there should be some "glow" on the act curtain before your show starts, otherwise the drape looks dead and uninviting. Light can be projected from above, below, or the sides. If you have an "open stage" (no curtain), use a warm glow in the middle of the set and a subtle highlight on some interesting bit of equipment— the chimes, music open on the piano, the vaudeville trunk that will later open to reveal a costume change, or your oversize logo against the back curtain or on the bass drum. Just before the show starts the curtain warmers fade to black and the general stage lighting takes over.

*"The size and intensity of the light can gently accentuate the emotional contour of the solo."*

### FOLLOW SPOT

With few exceptions, the light of the follow spot should "find" a soloist before we hear her sing. The size and intensity of the light can gently accentuate the emotional contour of the solo: the light expands toward the climax, but narrows to a pin spot (just outlining the face) near the end of a quiet, intense song. Size of the light must be rehearsed so the soloist knows what size of gestures will fall within the light.

Standard focus: 1) A circle of light beginning at chest level in which the face is the center of the circle. 2) The bottom edge of light is just below the waist— the face is in the upper third of the light. 3) The entire body is illuminated— the bottom edge of the light falls just in front of the feet.

Be aware of the less-intense edge of most follow spots and be sure that the soloist's forehead and hair fall within the bright part of the light. When the final gesture includes fully outstretched arms (either up or out), be sure the light is wide enough to illuminate the hands and fingertips!

The lighting designer must be careful that the general stage light or background color doesn't negate the intensity or color of the follow-spot. If the background is too well lit, a less intense spotlight can actually make the soloist disappear!

## MASK

Create a solid looking "set" out of your spindle-legged, see-through risers. Use eight inch strips of masonite or cloth or cardboard to cover the open front of a standard choral riser. The mask may be neutral beige or gray, or your school or group color or may change for each event in your season. For a splash, try reflective mylar, or aluminum foil, or fancy wallpaper, or a black-and-white keyboard design.

## OPEN THE HOUSE

The "house" is the part of the theater where the audience sits. "House" may also refer to the audience itself. You'll open the box office for ticket sales long before you actually let the audience into the house. In fact, to create an aura of excitement for your show, let the audience past the ticket window, but not *into* the seating area, until a crowd forms in the lobby. Many people in close proximity create a stir, a sense of anticipation. The ideal situation is to create a small "log-jam" of people at the doors even after the house is opened, so each arriving audience member comes into the bustling crowd, instead of passing through an empty lobby. Of course, the trick is to time this so you don't have to hold the curtain for 15 minutes while the ushers seat the audience you've held too long!

*"To create an aura of excitement for your show, let the audience past the ticket window, but not into the seating area, until a crowd forms in the lobby."*

## OPERATORS

A sound technician should always be present at the sound board throughout your show. Mics that aren't being used should be turned off. This allows a little more volume in the ones that *are* being used. As microphone stands are moved or adjusted, the mics should be turned off to avoid amplified rattling and bumping. It isn't necessary to have the mixing board smack in the middle of the house, but try to avoid locations where the sound is downright bad— under the balcony, in the orchestra pit under the stage, or behind glass windows in the back of the theatre.

The followspot operator must rehearse cues and know the size and color of spot you want in every instance. Even if your stage lighting is only the-front-bank-of-gym-lights, *someone* needs to know which switches to throw when. That someone becomes an integral part of

*"Doesn't your principal always lurk around the exit doors during a concert? What do you do when he leans against the light switch?"*

your technical support crew. (Doesn't your Principal always lurk around the exit doors during the concert? Who is responsible when he accidently leans against the master switch and brings up the houselights?) Important assignment!

Another "someone" must be in charge of opening and closing the curtain at just the right time and at just the right tempo. If you're the director, you ought to be too busy. The end girl on the first riser, who would always have to make a late entrance and an early exit, isn't a good choice either.

## PIANO LIGHT

Too often a last minute afterthought. Place the light so it doesn't shine in the eyes of the audience. Place it so unwanted light doesn't spill from the pit onto the stage. A layer or two of blue "gel" masks the light, but leaves enough to read the music.

## REHEARSAL SCHEDULE

Post a tentative schedule on your Call Board, and make a *big deal* about calling attention to revisions. As the date of your show approaches, post notices of tech rehearsals and dress rehearsal all over school to draw attention to the preparation for your special event. (Do this in addition to the posters and flyers you've got up everywhere!)

To encourage a sense of anticipation and "time-grows-short" in your rehearsal room, put up a long calendar/chart that lists all your repertoire and rehearsal days 'til curtain. After each rehearsal, check off the numbers that were rehearsed that day. Everyone will see DAY ONE approaching and, hopefully, also see progress and growth toward the total package.

## A SHORT BETWEEN THE EARPHONES

Never say this aloud, and realize that everybody has bad moments. But this is sometimes the "inexplicable" technical glitch that explains how it is possible for a soloist to step up to a mic—as rehearsed—and sing two or three measures before the sound comes through the speakers or before the followspot finds him.

## SPECIAL EFFECTS

Special effects are great fun, but use them sparingly and well. An effect must really *enhance* the number in which it is used, or it isn't worth the time and trouble it takes to set it up and rehearse it. Special effects are fun if unexpected. They are useless if they cause a stage wait while you drag on a bunch of equipment or wait for the black lights to warm-up.

## WARM UP

This goes along with *Sneak Attack*. Vocal warm-ups should take place well off stage (or on-stage *before* the house opens). Instrumentalists should tune and warm-up off stage once the audience begins to arrive. Electronic instruments and the sound system should be turned on, tested, pre-set, and LEFT ON until the show is *over*. (Once the electricity is running through all those wires, don't risk the unpredictable power surge that happens when you throw the switch.)

On the other hand, outdoors, at a shopping mall, or any place you need to attract an audience as you go, it can be a good idea to pique interest by having sound checks and instrumentalists warming-up on stage right up until show time.

*"The sound system should be turned on and left on until the show is over."*

*Technicians of every sort contribute as much to the success of your show as the featured center-stage spotlight soloist.*

# 17. PRINTED PROGRAMS

The primary purpose of a printed program is to list the routine of the show for the audience, right? Wrong.

A symphony orchestra program lists two works before intermission and the featured masterwork that makes up the entire second part of the program. A formal college choir program lists several works which will be performed in historical order. But *your* show will feature six or seven choirs performing sixteen or twenty numbers, not to mention the featured and incidental soloists.

Anything can happen between final proofs and opening curtain. Guest soloists can't come, finger cymbals fall down behind trophy case, Kindergarten "icicles" can't get their dunce caps on in time, producer/director (you!) changes mind at last minute.

No one can read a program in the dark, anyway.

The purpose of your printed program is to offer people something to do while they wait for the curtain to go up and to give them one more thing to kick around the kitchen counters for a few days following the show. Of course you list all the vital statistics concerning the show, but your printed program is primarily a public relations tool, an educational instrument, and the first volley of the publicity campaign for your next event!

*"Your printed program is the first volley of the publicity campaign for your next event."*

## ANTICIPATION

Picture yourself all dressed up in your old school letter sweater. In one hand, your stadium blanket; in the other, your "Let's Go South" pennant. Now, load the family in the car and drive out to the stadium for the big opening game! The pep band is playing and everyone is really excited. You find your seats, open your souvenir program and read:

> **SOUTHERN WARRIORS DROP OPENER TO COOLIDGE**
> First half of play will belong to Coolidge as the Cardinals will dominate the field. Coolidge will score on their first possession with a twenty-four yard touchdown pass by Mark Lemke. The extra point will be good. Lemke will throw a second touchdown pass in the second quarter and, with a two-point conversion, the score will stand 15-0.

During half-time, the Warrior band will play a Salute to Stevie Wonder.

In the fourth quarter, the Warriors will take the ball forty-two yards down field to set up the only Southern TD. Quarterback Carl Miner will find receiver Ronnie Bowen open in the end-zone for a six yard touchdown pass. The extra-point attempt will fail. Final score: Coolidge 15, Southern 6. See you next week at Watanabe High!

Kinda takes the wind out of your sails... Just as well round up your kids and head home *before* the National Anthem! For the Coolidge fans, where is the excitement that comes from the unexpected and un-known? Don't do the same thing to *your* fans at the Fall Choral Concert. You can go ahead and list the songs alphabetically under the heading "Tonight's Program Will Be Selected From The Following:" but don't give away just exactly who-does-what-and-when. (I think some directors change the printed routine *on purpose,* knowing that the audience will rattle their programs trying to find their place on the list, and drown-out an ill prepared number! What do you think?)

## PROGRAM NOTES

The printed program is the appropriate place for background information concerning each work. Some *succinct* remarks concerning the composer, historical significance, and signposts toward directed listening are all good. Don't, however, turn your program into a six page musicological thesis justifying the development of architechtonic compositional techniques in light of the socio-economic climate in fifteenth-century Flanders!

Include things like a little personal information on the training and aspirations of your featured soloists— it brings your show and performers closer to home for your audience. Don't expect everyone to read every word. A brief, spoken introduction from the stage makes the audience feel *involved* in the program.

*"The program is the appropriate place for background information but don't turn your program into a six-page musicological thesis."*

## PUBLICITY

Here is your chance to list the Five W's of upcoming events, and to use your list of "buzz words" to begin to establish image and character! "The Vespers Concert, to be performed at twilight on December 9th, will be an elegant, candlelit evening of seasonal favorites. Watch for further announcements concerning limited availability of tickets."

## PUBLIC RELATIONS

You are already aware of the importance of the personal contact between the audience, your box office personnel, and ushers. The printed program is the first audience contact by the performers. Be sure it represents you well.

Why not include a letter of welcome from the director, or the choir president, or the superintendent, or booster club secretary? "Welcome. We're glad you're here. Share our pride in, and wholehearted support for, these aspiring young entertainers." (Write this out ahead of time and hand it to your principal to sign!)

Acknowledgement of all the individuals and organizations who contribute to the success of your show are more effective when written down. For this show, the sixth-assistant custodian only unlocked the broom closet so *you* could sweep the stage, but once he sees his name in print, he might set up the folding chairs for your next show. Don't limit your list of thank-you's!

Your printed program is also a good place for an explanation of the "New Piano Fund" or "Director's Circle" support group. During the show, the Master of Ceremonies can refer to the subject without a *long* explanation and plea— "for details, and the address to send your generous donation, look in your program!"

*"The printed program is the first audience contact with your show. Be sure it represents you well."*

## SOUVENIR PROGRAM

If you perform a lot out in the community, you need a souvenir program. If you're going on tour, you need a souvenir program. If you need to raise extra funds by selling advertising space, you need a souvenir program.

If you have already developed a good publicity packet, then most of your work is done. Your expanded program should include your repertoire list for the season, selected program notes for unusual feature numbers, short biographical sketches of the performers and director, acknowledgement of both your on-the-road and home-base support staff, and a blurb about your school and music program.

A tour program traditionally names the place and date of the First Performance of your current show and includes reviews, highlights, and quotes.

If you go all out and *sell* your program book, it must have:

1) Visual Appeal - especially the front cover - strong graphics, photographs, and color.

2) Weight— as many pages as possible on the heaviest-stock paper you can afford.

The idea is to catch the eye with something that *looks* appealing from a distance (photographs, artwork, color, and distinctive typeface), and to put something in the hand of the potential buyer that *feels* heavy and important.

Aural memory is often short; visual memory is long. Your souvenir book lengthens and strengthens the impact and impression of your performance. Include photographs of rehearsals, performances, performers, tech crew in action, and a few special candids to project your fun-loving "Youth-of-America" image.

## VITAL STATISTICS

You know all of these— name of show, date and *year* (ten years from now, you will have forgotten), place of performance, and the *director's name.* Take advantage of the space to add "bigness" to your production— list performers and soloists, accompanists, crew, and everyone who helped with lights, sound, costumes, publicity, box office, decor, etc.

*"Catch the eye with something that* looks *appealing and feels heavy and important."*

# 18. PACING

**ABRUPT ENDING**

A lot of up-tempo numbers drive straight through to the end without slowing the underlying rhythmic or harmonic pulse. They end, suddenly, on a staccato eighth or quarter-note. Emotionally shocking, but not good for drawing the immediate, sustained applause you count on at the end of a set or show.

**APPLAUSE**

As you present your show, monitor audience reaction by being aware of the *sound* and *character* of their applause:

1) **Immediacy of Response** How long (or short) the delay from the end of the music to the first applause. At the end of an emotional ballad, hope for a long moment of silence as the effect "sinks in." The same silence after a production number says that you have let the audience's attention wander.

*"The next time you have a small audience, take a moment to rehearse their applause."*

2) **Depth of Sound** This is obvious: more people clapping more vigorously makes a bigger, deeper roar. Be aware whether the response is immediately unanimous, or if the *few* seem to "drag" the rest of the audience into applause. (*Faster* clapping has more depth. A small studio audience sounds bigger if each person claps faster. Next time you find yourself facing a small audience, take a moment to "rehearse" their applause— they'll love being let in on one of the 'tricks of the trade!')

3) **Duration Before the Peak** Applause follows a certain predictable contour. A moment of building enthusiasm (short or long), then a sustain toward a peak (hopefully long!), and finally a decay of energy (either abrupt or reluctant).

There are a few tricks to "milking" sustained applause. a) Delay the conductor's bow: first, turn your head over your shoulder to "listen" to the applause; then, turn to face the audience in modest disbelief; *finally,* bow and hold the position for a moment. b) Delay acknowledging soloists and accompanist; but not too long! Once the peak has passed, it isn't fair to force the audience to "rev-up" again. (From the performer's point of view, there is nothing worse than bowing in the face of dying applause.) c) Tease the audience: If you have established a good rapport, you can cup one hand to your ear as if to say, "I can't hear quite enough applause." Smile and nod agreement when the sound swells. Be sure you're "milking" applause only for a performance that really deserves it— the audience will know the difference between encouragement and begging.

## CHINESE ACT

"On Too Long." How many times have you gone to a show or concert where every number dragged on and on? Past the point of enjoyment, past interest, beyond endurance! Are *you* ever guilty of singing every verse and chorus just because that's the way the arrangement is written? (Once the parts are learned, we can fill more performance time without much more rehearsal.)

The world's attention span is geared to T.V. time— five minute sequences of scenes that vary in length from a few seconds to a few minutes. These sequences are interrupted by a series of thirty-second bursts of "mini-shows" (commercials). At least every thirty minutes there is time to get up and stretch and raid the refrigerator! Attention spans are short.

Another challenge is that the range and timbre of the choral instrument is somewhat limited, especially for young singers. It is hard to sustain interest based on sound alone. Professional performers, both live and in recordings, are able to play tricks to sustain our interest. They can modulate, one chorus at a time, up off the scale. They can add strings and horns to underscore each successive verse. They finally throw in the electronic Music of the Spheres and an echo chamber for the last chorus!

Of course, well crafted compositions and arrangements add interest through harmonic growth, texture changes, and rhythmic variation. But, even so, twenty-five untrained singers and a spinet piano will be hard-pressed to recreate the effect of a four minute recording!

At least, let "On Too Long" have a place in the back of your mind.

*"Professional performers play tricks to sustain our interest: electronic music of the Spheres and an echo chamber for the last chorus."*

## SHOWSTOPPER

Some numbers are so effective that they can't be followed by *anything.* You'll probably know if you have a "showstopper" in the routine of your show. Everything will grind to a halt for endless, thunderous applause, and it will take the audience a long time to settle back into the mood for hearing the next number.

Often, big bombastic numbers are showstoppers, but beautiful ballads and inspirational solos can have the same effect. Your *planned* show, whether a 20-minute segment or a two-hour production, ideally clips along at a predetermined pace—no delays for position changes, equipment moves, nor for extended applause. But, the reaction to a true showstopper must be allowed to run its course.

The best thing to program after a showstopper is an absolute *contrast*— solo to ensemble, accompanied to acappella, light-hearted to dead-serious. Further, break the emotional continuum by some spoken words on a new subject. The next singer can introduce her solo, or the Master of Ceremonies can acknowledge the Mayor in the audience. The break allows the audience to come down out of the clouds and *pay attention* to the rest of the show.

### STAGE WAIT

Ten seconds of "dead air" on radio or T.V. is enough time for you to lose interest and change the channel. A live audience is captive in the theatre, so they can't switch channels, but they can and *will* 'tune out!' Don't let this happen to you.

Most of the moments when nothing is happening are a result of neglect of tight pacing. The downbeat *could* have come five seconds earlier, but the conductor was willing to wait while a few people rearranged their music. Willing to wait while chairs and stands were adjusted. Willing to wait until a breathless hush settled over the audience.

*Don't be willing to wait!* It is a sign that *you* aren't in control of the show. The accompanist is in control, the soloist is in control—but *you* are not in control. Any job expands to fill the time allotted to it, but all those little on-stage jobs that can delay your show will also *contract!* Insist on contraction. You'll be amazed how quickly and efficiently things will happen when you expect it:

**Stage Director's Rule Number One:** "To clear the stage after a mob scene, *demand* a four-second exit to a totally clear stage, then *run it 'til it works."*

**Corollary to Stage Director's Rule Number One:** "Never look back-stage to see how deep the bodies are piled in the wings!"

*"Never look back-stage to see how deep the bodies are piled in the wings!"*

Your accompanist may have to play three bars from memory while the page-turner adjusts the next score. The next soloist may have to step into position, and adjust the microphone, during the preceding applause. The pace of the show is everyone's job. After all, you've invited a houseful of guests for an evening of *music*. Don't make them sit through the preparations.

## TRANSITIONS

Sometimes major shuffling between numbers can't be avoided. Some can be covered by a few words from the Master of Ceremonies, some can become part of the choreography of your show, and some can be underscored by transition music.

The best, most logical, transition music is the introduction to the *next* song. Second choice would be some sort of recurring "theme" music that is played under each major transition.

A distant third choice is to reprise the theme of the just-finished number. Psychologically, we're finished with the *preceding* emotion. We want a *new* feeling, a new color, new tempo, texture, and key. A transition should be in the character of the *next*, unknown number, not the tired old previous one. You *can* tack a reprise onto a big production number, but, in that case, you are "topping" the number with one last blast, not merely limping away from it.

## STANDARD TIME FRAME

Based on audience attention span, and the demands of repetition and contrast, here are a few "target" times for a medley or musical variety show:

Your basic, run-of-the-mill, *standard number* runs between 1:20 (one minute and twenty seconds) and 2:40— enough time for a verse or two and a couple of choruses with a key change.

A dandy *feature* that really showcases a special talent of the ensemble or a soloist will hold our attention in the range of 3:00 to 4:00+. (The audience *will*, of course, sit still longer than this, but there is a difference between the hush of rapt attention and the stony silence of polite endurance!)

Anything longer must be considered a GEM. Something entirely different from anything else in the program. Like a gem in a necklace, everything that surrounds it must complement the gem. Attention is focused on the gem, because it asks for (and deserves) extended consideration and concentration.

Finally, sprinkle your presentation with short THROWAWAYS, just :40 to 1:00 in length, that tease the audience to the edge of their seats in anticipation of what's to come or in contrast to what's come before.

> *"A transition should be in the character of the next, unknown number, not the tired old previous one."*

# 19. PERSONAL TOUCH

### USHERS

Your ticket-takers, program-hander-outers, and ushers are the first *personal contact* the audience has with your show. *(The Show* actually began way back with the mood and anticipation created by your publicity, and continued as the audience approached your theatre, passed under your 'marquee,' and entered your lobby.) Ushers should be well-briefed and rehearsed, well-dressed— or in costume if it would enhance your pre-show atmosphere— and well-mannered. The usher's smile or frown sets the mood for the entire evening; they need to be aware of their invaluable contribution to the overall success of *The Show.*

### GLARING PROBLEMS

Something *will* go wrong. Count on it and be prepared! Even the best rehearsed song can falter, a dancer falls, a singer faints, a dog wanders on stage, Aunt Edith gets carried away and starts to sing along. In the case of minor "glitches" your performers should be trained to pick themselves up and go right on with the show. But, when things simply collapse, the best thing to do is stop, call attention to the problem (you can't *really* fool the audience— you shouldn't want to), and assure them that everything will be OK. Simply say, "Gosh, this never happened in rehearsal. You won't mind if we start again so you can hear the best we can do!" Every audience *wants* to hear and see a terrific performance; they can be very forgiving. Then either go back and "pick up the pieces," or forge right ahead ("You'll want to come back to our Spring show to see if we figure out how to solve this problem!"), leaving the problem spot to fade in everyone's memory.

### FIRST NAMES

When you introduce singers on stage, it is warm and un-stuffy to introduce them by their first names. You establish a personal rapport with the audience: "Mary... Cousin Henry's youngest daughter is named Mary, too; why, these performers are just like the kids next door!" Of course it works if your group is "down-home," but even for a slick and glitzy group it helps to counteract that unwelcome "aloof" feeling toward the audience.

> *"Every audience wants to hear and see a terrific performance; they can be very forgiving."*

## WELCOME

One of the best ways to get your administration involved in your program is to arrange for the principal, superintendent, or school board member to deliver a brief "welcome" in the middle of one of your shows. It gives the administrator a vested interest in the success and quality of your program, and demonstrates to the audience (and to you and your students) administrative support for your efforts.

## AN EVENING OF ENTERTAINMENT

Your performance has a lot in common with a dinner party. Guests have been invited. The purpose of the evening is shared enjoyment of a "main event." Time and energy have been spent planning, preparing, and presenting the main event. The main event is made up of a selected variety of smaller events or courses.

Picture, if you will, the following scene: We're invited to a formal dinner. Well, it's not something we usually do, but we decide to make an effort to clear our schedules and eagerly anticipate the *Special Event.* We arrive right on time and ring the doorbell. The door opens and we are ushered silently to places at the table. The host and hostess enter the dining room but acknowledge our greetings with only a smile and a nod. The dinner begins. The lady across the table, thinking the soup course to be some sort of chilled tomato puree, enjoys several large spoonfuls before being nudged and furtively asked to pass the Russian dressing. The food is all delicious, but the unusual main course is served in an exotic way. We're not sure which fork to use (or maybe a spoon, or is this finger-food?), but the glances of our equally confused fellow diners warn us that it would be inappropriate to ask. At last the endless and awkward meal comes to an end and we rush for the door, agreeing that we won't be quite so anxious to accept a future invitation.

> *"Hysterical guests charge the exit hoping to escape an evening of snobbish musical entertainment."*

I've never really experienced such a dinner (except for the Russian dressing incident), but I *have* watched equally hysterical guests charge the nearest exit hoping to escape an evening of snobbish musical entertainment to which they have eagerly accepted an invitation! Will they ever come back? What could we, as hosts and hostesses, have done to make their experience less uncomfortable?

The answer is PERSONAL TOUCH: Let your guests know they're welcome. Guide them through an unfamiliar experience. Develop an *audience-oriented* point-of-view.

### ROOTS

Our traditional approach to presenting a concert is based on the model of the Orchestra Concert: "The houselights dim, the conductor enters and leads the first major work, applause, he leaves the stage, houselights up, intermission, houselights dim, he comes back to conduct the second major work, applause, bows, houselights up, go home." It all works very well. Very formal, very impersonal. We have come to *witness* an event (the recreation of a few familiar works). It is hoped that we will "get into" the music, but we are not expected to get involved in the *event*.

Most school concerts, and certainly all variety concerts, are more nearly based on the Vaudeville Show: "Houselights dim, overture, master of ceremonies greets, tells jokes, asks questions (expects response), introduces acrobatic act, long-legged blonde presents title card, applause, introduction, dog act, applause, introduction, comedy skit, applause, introduction, poetry reading, applause, introduction, Headline Magician, applause, drawing for door prize, houselights up, go home." It also works very well. Very informal, very personal. We have come to be *part of* an event. We are expected to make a major contribution to the success of the evening.

Substitute "Girls Triple Trio," "Concert Choir," and "Freshman Chorus" for "Acrobats," "Poetry Reading," and "Dog Act," and our description transfers pretty neatly from the Vaudeville Theatre to the High School Gymtorium or Auditeria!

> *"Our traditional approach is based on the Orchestra Concert. Most school concerts are more nearly based on the Vaudeville Show."*

*This is a silly picture, but perhaps it makes a point: Too many musicians simply play or sing their music in a room — a spectator sport at best. Entertainers sincerely strive to fill a room with energy, always dedicated to audience enjoyment!*

# 20. MASTER OF CEREMONIES

*Personal Touch* is often assigned to one person who acts as the official "host" for the evening of entertainment. Of course the duties of "host" can be divided among a number of people— teachers, students, administrators— but the purpose and guidelines remain the same.

## RAPPORT

This is the primary objective of any M.C.; to establish a link across the footlights between performers and audience. Set the audience at ease. Remind them that this isn't T.V. and that they are expected to *participate*.

> *"Remind the audience that this isn't T.V.: they are expected to participate."*

## STYLE

Some occasions are formal; many are not. The comments of the M.C. can be "off the cuff" (though always considered and rehearsed), delivered 'by heart,' or read from notes (never try to *sneak* in reading notes— we all know what you're up to, so your act gets to be about faking instead of hosting.) The Master of Ceremonies is, by definition, a figure of authority. Think through what you *need* to share with the audience; be sure you've got all the names and dates and facts straight before you go on!

## PURPOSE

The role of the M.C. is (besides setting the audience at ease) to introduce, explain, direct our attention, and to establish scene, mood, or attitude. Comments may precede a number or a set of songs, or the explanation/introduction may follow. (Remember the element of surprise.) In planning the pace of a show, always take into consideration the purpose, length, and character of the M.C.'s comments.

## RELATED COMMENTS

A *Master of Ceremonies* will, of course, name performers, composers, and works, but can also focus "directed listening" by relating historical background, stylistic peculiarities, form, poetic interpretation, or translations. Other topics of discussion could include "our next performance," "our last major success," "the scholarship fund," or "our exciting summer project." The M.C. should have a few comments concerning current events, the weather, or "what we're missing on T.V. tonight" ready in case of an unexpected stage wait.

### TITLES

In a spoken introduction don't reveal the title of a well-known song. You destroy the wonderful moment of recognition as the first notes of the introduction sound or the murmur of appreciation as the familiar chorus begins!

*Quality is in the details. Rehearse the comments and pacing of the MC as diligently as the rest of your show.*

# EPILOGUE
## by
### John Jacobson

## 100% POSITIVE:
## THE ART OF ENTERTAINMENT
## FESTIVALS AND WORKSHOPS

*Let's face it, most of the people who will read this book are involved with entertainment in a voluntary community organization or an educational setting. Whatever the situation, through your hard work, the art is created. Now, what do you do with it?*

*I have told the story countless times. Yet, on a Sunday morning flight home after a weekend with five hundred Junior High performers, when I feel as though I can hardly lift an arm, to say nothing about repack my suitcase for another cross-country trek on Monday morning; my voice is raspy, my feet are throbbing, my social life is a disaster and I can't find my socks...Michelle keeps me going. More than the applause, the paycheck, the gratitude of the parents or even the music...Michelle is the reason that music education is the greatest place to be.*

*Fritz and I were conducting an "Art of Entertainment" festival in one of our favorite North Carolina destinations a few years ago. It was fairly typical for us, the combined choirs of four separate high schools gathered together for a three day festival that culminated in a Saturday night extravaganza with no holds barred. It included music from Mozart to Manilow, dance and staging of many styles, costumes, dialogue, lights and learning. A weekend to celebrate this generation and their participation in the arts.*

*In this situation the notes are learned before Fritz and I show up so that most of our time can be spent on interpretation and teaching the choreography. In other words, our job is to make the notes into music and the event into a "show." With three or four hundred students it's difficult to learn all of their names or the specific spectrum of their talents, so, mostly we sort of lump them all together, teach everybody everything and hope that, though exhausted, they will remember this weekend as one of the most positive events in their lives so far, with music as the focal point of those good feelings.*

*Thursday night is reserved, almost exclusively, for musical rehearsal with an hour or so at the end allotted to "get the kids moving". In this*

> *"Through your hard work, the art is created. Now, what do you do with it?"*

way they have an idea of what to expect for the next two days of long, strenuous hours with few breaks. So, it wasn't until about 8 p.m. that I had a turn to stand in front of the mass, lead them through some more physical warm-ups and introduce them to some of the moves that we would incorporate in the show we would be working on the next day. I love that rehearsal because everyone is so anxious to get moving and bodies and brains are still fresh. When we finished at around 9:15, I was enjoying the bustle of the excited students as they were deciding who was staying at whose home that night, laughing at a joke Fritz had made in the vocal rehearsal, and thinking to myself, "I can't believe we're going to try to accomplish all that we have planned by Saturday night." From behind I felt a gentle tug at my sleeve. Thinking that it was Fritz I turned around and said "O.K. Mr. Mountford, next week I'll teach the music and you handle the choreography." (An idle threat I assure you!) Instead, I found myself looking into the bright blue eyes of a beautiful girl named Michelle. Her face was so eager and her shyness so obvious that I immediately felt a pull at my heart, especially when I noticed that she stood with the help of crutches, the metal sort of permanent kind that attach below the elbows as if to say, "where Michelle goes, I go." Michelle had cerebral palsy.

"Mr. Jacobson...I mean John," soft-spoken Michelle spoke in a run-on sentence, obviously rehearsed, "I've learned every note of the music and I really want to be a part of The Art of Entertainment but, as you can see, some of the dancing is a little out of my league although I think I could do a good bit of it with the help of my crutches, but, if you'd rather I stayed out of it I'd surely understand. I'm a good singer you know."

"Yes Michelle, you are a good singer and this weekend is for anyone who loves music; you must be a part of The Art of Entertainment! When we work on choreography you do as much as you think you can and when the movement gets to be too much just sing, because, you are a wonderful singer", I blurted out in a run-on sentence of my own.

*"And on Saturday night, when the air was filled with the electricity that happens when performers meet an audience, Michelle was a dancer!"*

Friday morning arrived and for twelve grueling hours we took the students through their paces. Michelle was there. Saturday rolled around and it was another all "dance 'til you drop" day. Michelle was there again, in fact, she never left. Oh sure, sometimes it took her a little bit longer than the rest of the chorus to make it up the steps to the stage. There were times when the choreography called for the right hand to shoot straight up in the air and Michelle would barely lift hers from the handle of her crutch. Sometimes we swayed energetically from left to right and Michelle's movement was nearly imperceptible. But she sang! From her heart and soul, from head to toe Michelle sang. "She was a very good singer you know!" And, on Saturday night, when the air was filled with the electricity that happens when performers meet an audience, Michelle, too, put on her long white dress; for tonight...Michelle was a dancer!

When working in a professional performance situation the producer/ director has the authority and the luxury to seek out and find the exact performer for the role he has in mind. If he is casting WEST SIDE STORY he hunts far and wide for the tall, dark Italian tenor to play Tony. If he is casting ANNIE he looks for a precocious little redhead for the title role. We have all heard the nightmares of professional performers at auditions where the decision is made whether or not to consider a performer for a role the second they walk in the door. "Typing out" is an easy way of narrowing the field in a business too full of prospective performers. Too tall, too short, too fat, too thin, too blond, too bald, too, too,...are all used to eliminate from the cast of thousands and come up with the "ideal" ensemble.

In a professional situation this "weeding out" process is real and necessary. In secondary and elementary education it is not! In school, anyone with the courage, ambition and desire deserves a chance to step onto the stage and participate. In athletics, academics, auto mechanics and art, the classroom is the place for trying things out. It's the place for having experiences you may never have again, at least never so safely and with so much encouragement. In music theater and the rest of the arts we shouldn't limit the beauty of participation to the twenty-two inch waist, the clear complexion, the mother with the station wagon, or only the students who can afford the two-hundred dollar sequined gown. Can you imagine "typing out" beautiful, blue-eyed Michelle, the singer/ dancer?

*"In school, anyone with the courage, ambition and desire deserves a chance to step onto the stage and participate."*

We live in a very specialized world. I remember meeting a man once whose sole daily job was to dust off the light bulbs in an exclusive hotel lobby. Choices of vocation and avocation are pressed upon us from a very early age. But, arts in education is for everyone. The image conscious, two-hundred pound football player, the insecure wallflower, the overweight, the under-loved, the too tall, too short, too fat, too thin, too blond, too bald, too, too...deserve to find a place to belong in the music programs of our schools and communities. What a privilege we have to offer it to them. It can be the one thing in all of their lives that is 100% positive!

MUSIC EDUCATION...Where Everyone Is A Winner!?

100% Positive...What an interesting notion! Pollyanna? Perhaps. I don't think so. A group of professionals sat around a table with yellow notepads in front of them and years of experience in choral music education behind them. They were, in the opinions of many, the "best" and "most respected" in their field and, though humble, they realized that they had the opportunity to make a dent in their world.

**The objective:**

*"Create a universally acceptable scoring sheet to be used by themselves and other professionals involved in adjudicating choral competitions across the country. With this tool of standardization every ensemble in every contest would know in advance on what scale they would be judged. The percentage of the total score given for each category of what these professionals considered the essentials of a good musical endeavor would, at last, be consistent. From now on, competitors would know where the "real" priorities of "good" art lie. No more frustrations. No more misunderstandings. Let's set it once and for all."*

> **"Create a universally accepted scoring sheet to be used in adjudicating choral competitions across the country."**

**The dialogue begins:**

*"Let's start with a perfect score of 100 and break it down from there."*

*"A sound idea! That sure makes keeping track of who's winning a lot easier."*

*"I think we all agree that musicality is the most important category and ought to be placed first on the list."*

*"You mean before vocal technique?"*

*"Perhaps you're right. Vocal technique certainly is important. How about putting it first and following up with musicality."*

*"But what about diction and breath support? Don't they deserve scores of their own or are they simply sub-categories under technique?"*

*"Diction, a sub-category!?!?"*

*"O.K., O.K., let's give 20 points each for vocal technique, diction and musicality, breaking down the musicality portion with 6 points each for timbre and tone, and eight points for dynamics."*

*"Are you suggesting that we lump the men's section in with the women's and come up with one score on tone quality?"*

*"Oh, you're right. O.K., 3 points for women's tone and 3 for men's, 3 for women's timbre and 3 for men's, with 4 each for the dynamics of each group. Or should we judge each section separately so that the sopranos get 1.5, altos 1.5, tenors 1.5 and basses 1.5, except of course where there were eight points to divide in which case it would be an even 2,2,2 and 2!?"*

*"Sounds simple so far!"*

*"Doesn't anybody care anything about pitch?"*

*"Surely we have to be able to give separate scores for separate songs! Some groups could sing very musically on a pop ballad and fall completely flat on an English madrigal!"*

*"Good point! Let's have separate scores for each song and then average them up for the final picture!"*

*"Hey, what about choreography?"*

*"O.K. I feel strongly that the choice of repertoire is worth at least 15 points. There's nothing that disgusts me more than inappropriate repertoire!"*

*"Hear! Hear!"*

*"Is that a flat 15 points or should we make sub-categories such as programming, pacing, etc.?"*

*"Of course! How about 5 points each for programming, pacing, variety, and difficulty?"*

*"But that's 20 points!"*

*"Fine! 20 points it is!"*

*"Have we talked yet about transitions?"*

*"Yeah, and what about choreography?"*

*"'STAGE WEIGHT!!!"*

*"No problem. Let's throw in an even 10 points for transitions, with sub-categories for entrance and exit."*

*"Great! More sub-categories!"*

*"Now, what about costumes?"*

*"You mean now we have to be fashion critics?"*

*"Look, if I sell nine thousand dollars worth of grapefruit to buy sequined gowns I certainly want it to count for something!"*

> *"Look, if I sell $9,000 worth of grapefruit to buy sequined gowns I certainly want it to count for something."*

*"What do costumes have to do with good music?"*

*"Don't ask me, ask my Music Mothers!"*

*"I like costumes!"*

*"I hate grapefruit!"*

"Easy folks. O.K., 5 points for costumes."

"FIVE POINTS!? That's not worth two crates of stale M&M's!!!"

"That's show biz!!!"

"Is anybody gonna talk about choreography?"

"Alright, alright! You dancer types are so annoying sometimes!"

"Let's see. We've used 20 points each for vocal technique, diction and musicality. Plus 20 points for repertoire, broken up into sub-categories of programming, pacing, variety and difficulty. With the 10 points for transitions and 5 points for costumes we've used up 95 points so far. I guess that that leaves us with a nice plug nickel to cover staging, choreography, facial expression, show concept, design and emotional appeal!"

"Sounds good to me! Let's go get 'em!"

O.K,. O.K., So I got a little carried away! But, the scenario is not all that unrealistic. What is a really fair assessment of what is good and what isn't when it comes to the arts? Who is confident enough of their taste to sit alone or on a panel and give one work of art a blue ribbon and another a red? One a gold medal and another a bronze? Who can put a numerical value on art? Who would want to?

> **"What is good and what isn't when it comes to the arts? Who is confident enough to put a numerical value on art?"**

In the past few years many of our choral music programs have centered around a few dates in the spring of the year. We pile our students, risers, microphones, stage crews, costumes and cheering sections onto a bus still smelly from a Friday night away game and drive any number of miles to pit our singers against the "best of show" from other schools. Before the advent of the "show" and "jazz" phase we did the same with our concert choirs and madrigal ensembles. In many cases we now do both. We sing. We dance. We cheer. We execute our set-up, take down, entrance, bow and exit in an exact 19 minutes and 55 seconds to beat the twenty minute time limit. We've got our one minute and thirty second opener in a feeling of "one." We follow with something in a nice bouncy "two" feel and stun the audience with our tasteful ballad third. It's time for a little humor or at least a novelty number so they'll barely be able to distinguish us from the other groups. They'll remember our flash pots, our acrobat or our mascot pig who tap danced to the tune of "Anything Goes!" Quickly, bring the judges to tears with the inspirational penultimate number complete with sign language and $CO_2$. Bookend the entire event with a thirty second reprise of the opening number, bump *off a clever bow and get off the stage. Don't worry, you're well rehearsed, fully choreographed, stage crew with complementary costumes and matching whisk brooms will deftly clear the debris!*

*"O.K. O.K. So I got carried away again! So take a few points off for melodrama!"*

*The crazy thing about all this competition commentary is that we really like the whole event! Me too! Or at least 95% of it. We love to see the students from many different schools get together and perform for each other. I like to hear them cheer each other on. We all think it's important to work hard to achieve a degree of excellence you never thought you could accomplish as an individual or as a group. A competition is often the kind of motivation young people respond to. That's one reason that athletics have been so popular in our schools for so long. We love the learning that happens. We get ideas from other groups that we can later go home and try for ourselves. We meet other people. We make new friends. We share our work and our art with other people who understand and appreciate what it took for us to get there. Like I said, 95% of what makes up a choral competition is really terrific!*

*"95% of what makes up a choral competition is really terrific! But, in the end, somebody loses. Is any of that worth even 5%?"*

*But, in the end, after a marvelous day of learning and sharing, praising and caring, somebody wins and somebody loses. One group is victorious and all the others are something less! And for what?! For another brass pin to tack on a letter sweater? For another plaque to cover the chips on the choir room wall? For a parade of parents to cheer us home or another eight foot trophy that someone has to dust off every other year?!*

*Is any of that worth even 5%?!*

*Granted, many competitions are run in such a classy fashion that the actual win itself is practically insignificant. Most directors have an adequate grip on perspective and stress that the trophy is not the real reason for going on stage. But, if that's the case...Why have trophies at all?*

*If what we do as music educators is produce an "art", then how are we to distinguish what is rewardable and what is not? Should a school of three-thousand students with a fourteen-thousand dollar choral budget be pitted against a school of two-hundred where the lead tenor is also the middle linebacker of the football team and the first saxophone in the marching band? Should the women in an ensemble be marked down if one person's stockings don't match or if all of their shoes aren't beige? Should the judge's scoring sheets be so specific that instead of encouraging creativity we encourage the creation of "clones of the kingdom?" Should the overweight student be left home because they detract from* the perfect Chorus Line look of your ensemble? Shall we design our show after last year's winner so that every group has red dresses this year? Or, should we try to please the judge on the left who we know has a weakness for Gilbert and Sullivan?

Is the group that uses a hot shot, East Coast professional choreographer on the same scoring system as the choir whose members design the staging themselves? Is a group that decides to do a speech chorus instead of a ballad disqualified, or a group that can't decide if they're "jazz" or "show" not invited? Shall we pit Mozart against Beethoven, Twain against Shakespeare, Chagall against Degas, Picasso against Rembrandt and decide who is the best artist?

Competition is a wonderful thing. Good grief! America is practically founded on the grounds that healthy, or even ruthless, competition is what makes us grow with quality. Learning how to win and how to lose with grace are crucial lessons for all people to learn. So...let's learn it in business. Let's learn it in athletics and politics, science and industry, "The Wheel of Fortune" and "Trivial Pursuit!" But, for the sake of Michelle...of Bobby and Steven and Mary and Jenny and...and...Let's let excellence be our trophy! Let's let every dreaming "artist" be a 100% winner!

> **"Let's let excellence be our trophy! Let's let every dreaming 'artist' be a 100% winner!"**

Well, it's easy to criticize, especially when you don't have a skeptical administration or a hard-to-please board of education to convince that worthy success really is being generated by the Fine Arts Department. A trophy is something that everyone can recognize as a concrete symbol of your good work. There's nothing criminal about tooting your own horn once in a while.

Fritz and I would be the first to say "Go for it!" if the choice for your performers was to participate in a competition, or stay home. Remember, 95% of the event will be a wonderful experience for all of you. Fortunately, however, you do have some choices.

Here are some examples of other types of organized entertainment options that may suit your particular requirements. Each of them is adaptable to all levels of experience and support. Each of them also has education and artistic quality as its goal, with "The Art Of Entertainment" as its vehicle, and excellence as its trophy.

### 1. THE ART OF ENTERTAINMENT CHORAL FESTIVAL

In one of the most successful formats for a choral festival, several performing organizations gather at one facility for approximately two or two-and-a-half days. The culminating event is a showcase featuring each of the ensembles individually and in a mass performing cast. The size of the group is determined generally by the size of the facility with anywhere from one-hundred to four-or-five-hundred working splendidly! Often a "guest" conductor and choreographer are invited to run the festival with the "producers" of each ensemble sharing the duties of host, section leaders, housing and other logistics coordinators, etc. The music to be performed ought to be as eclectic as possible, including many styles, or theming the event around a unifying topic, i.e. patriotic, seasonal, or so on. The schedule of the event could go something like this:

### Several months in advance:
The host directors communicate with the guest clinicians and chose music that they feel appropriate to the occasion. The individual directors order the music and begin rehearsing it with their groups so that by the time the event arrives the notes and lyrics are memorized. The guest conductor is invited to "make music" from these learned notes and lyrics. You probably wouldn't want to bring in somebody special and then expect them to pound notes.

Of course the individual groups are at the same time rehearsing their own individual repertoire so that it is ready for performance by the time the festival begins. There will be little time to rehearse that individual material with so much mass work to be done during the festival's two-and-a-half days. It is generally found that five to ten mass numbers are feasible depending on their difficulty and on the amount of staging that is intended. Those numbers along with one or two from each separate group will make for a nice performance at the end of the festival.

A couple of weeks prior to the festival it may or may not be feasible to gather the participating schools together for an evening rehearsal. This will serve as an early motivator for all as they begin to get acquainted with each other and take stock of what needs attention before the festival dates.

### Festival Day One (Thursday after school):
All of the performers gather at the festival site for a vocal rehearsal. The guest clinicians are introduced and the work begins. A capable accompanist who will be at every rehearsal to handle changes, modifications and any general musical whims of the conductors is crucial. Now the teamwork is really put into motion. Everyone's responsibilities are spelled out and everyone looks for ways that they can help tailor the show to this unique group and make the event more and more positive. This rehearsal usually goes from about 4 p.m. to 9 p.m. with some breaks left to the director's discretion. Most of the time is spent on the vocal aspects of the show with perhaps an hour or so at the end to "get everyone moving" with some choreography.

*"Everyone looks for ways to tailor the show to this group and make the event more and more positive."*

# 100% Positive

> "Being good is fun and being good takes hard work. They have experienced the privilege of being an entertainer and found it worth the effort."

### Day 2 (Friday):  9 a.m. to 9 p.m. or thereabouts:

Sing, dance, pound out details.  Break into sectionals if need be.  Work, work, work.  Being good is fun and being good takes hard work.  Alternate between vocal rehearsals and choreography lessons, combining the two when you feel you can.  Exhausting, thrilling, "competing" for excellence.

### Day 3 (Saturday, performance day):

The morning is dedicated to drilling what you worked on Friday and bringing up to date the students who missed Friday night's rehearsals to play in an athletic event.  Polish solos.  Work out transitions.  By noon full rehearsals have resumed.  Choral and staging clinicians work in tandem to finish teaching final staging and musical choices.  By about 4:00 a full run-through has begun with lights, orchestra and all of the elements falling into place with an all-out effort by everyone involved.  Rehearsals continue right up to the time that the doors open and the audience is let in.  The performers gulp their sack lunches, fix their hair and make-up, don their costumes and are ready for the big performance.  It's been proven that in such an intense rehearsal situation, with so much information absorbed by the performers in such a short time, the shorter the break between the final run-through and the final performance the better.  The performers hardly have time to forget anything.  Sure, they'll be exhausted mentally and physically.  But adrenaline, encouraged by a live audience and the thrill of performing in such a unique cast, will provide more than sufficient energy for this special occasion.

When the performance is over, the different groups have seen and heard their peers perform, and they have performed as a single unit.  They have been able to learn new music and choreography.  They have compared their efforts to the efforts of their friends and discovered that it's "O.K." for everyone to be good in their own way.  They have learned that it takes an almost super-human effort to make a show a success; it doesn't "just happen!"  They have worked harder than they have ever worked before.  They have experienced the privilege of being an entertainer and found it worth the effort.  Every one of them!

### 2.  KICK-OFF PERFORMANCES

A second highly successful format that is equally rewarding and motivational places the performance as the kick-off to the festival with the workshop following.  For instance, the performing groups from several schools gather at one host facility on a Friday night.  They invite a guest clinician or several to join them, or they simply do it on their own.  This evening, each ensemble performs 20 to 30 minutes of material that

138   Epilogue

they have perfected over the preceding weeks. The clinician gives constructive criticism into a tape recorder for the "producers" to listen to and consider at a later time. Sometimes the clinician will even join each group on stage after their performance to give comments for all to hear and discuss. Or, the performances are executed in a continuous and more formal manner for a mixed audience.

The next day the groups gather in their rehearsal clothes after a night spent sharing each other's homes and making new friends. The day is spent learning about The Art of Entertainment from the guest clinicians. Part of the day could be devoted to choreography and part to choral, or a specific topic could be addressed each year. The performers could even have a time to discuss last night's performances with helpful observations and comments of likes and dislikes, always keeping in mind a respect for each other and The Art of Entertainment.

### 3. "ALL-STAR" CAST

Another successful festival arrangement is perhaps a bit more selective than the first two, but equally stimulating for those involved. In this situation a few, or several, members of a performing group are selected to represent their cast at a one or two day workshop. The students gather together much like the first Art Of Entertainment Festival discussed above. A designated conductor/choreographer/clinician works with their "all-star" cast on music that may or may not be presented in a culminating performance. Although each school does not get to have everybody involved directly, the students that do participate are expected to go back to their groups and pass along what they have learned. This is much like the traditional "All-State" or "Honors" choruses have operated. Directly and indirectly, through their representatives, scores of interested performers are positively affected by this sort of gathering.

### 4. JOINT CONCERTS

A very simple way to share your art is to organize a joint concert with a school or organization near or far from you. Each group has a chance to perform for the other and for members of the community of the host group. It is relatively easy to do a couple of combined numbers to top off the show with little rehearsal time. Again, you can share each other's homes, schools and art, making new friends and experiencing a new artistic adventure all at the same time. Some groups have actually gone on tour doing joint concerts with several schools along the way. They have discovered that there are opportunities to be enjoyed that are actually impossible on their own. They need each other for their art! Healthy competition, great learning experience, fine art and everybody wins!

*"Students go back and pass along what they have learned: healthy competition, great learning experience, fine art and everybody wins!"*

### 5. THE COMMUNITY SING

How many times after a show have the parents and townspeople come up to you and said things like, "Gee, it looks like so much fun!". "I wish they would have offered opportunities like that when I was in school!" or "It made me want to jump up, sing and dance right along with you!"

Well, why not make their wishes come true? What better way to pull a community together than through music?

Invite the local church choirs to join together to form a community chorus. Include the local Sweet Adelines or even the jug band from the retirement center to join with the elementary, Junior High, and High School performing groups for a performance to remember! Every ensemble can do a few minutes of their own and conclude with a couple of mass numbers. Very often you may have more people on stage than in the audience. But, in this case that would be a roaring success! How exciting to have moms, dads, and grandparents singing and dancing along-side their sons, daughters and grandchildren! Once a year, once a decade, once in a lifetime, music can bring everybody together! Now...that's an art!

*"You may have more people on stage than in the audience. But, that would be a roaring success."*

### 6. SOUNDS LIKE LOVE

At a church in Minnesota seven-hundred young people gather for a weekend. The time is spent in fellowship, choral rehearsals, motivational and instructional workshops ranging from improvisational drama to dealing with drugs. For some of the youth this is the only organized chorus of which they've ever been a part.

With seven-hundred comrades the pressure is off to always stand out as an individual, and the motivation is on to relish the thrill of singing and dancing with unbridled heart and soul. Every note is difficult to perfect in this kind of arrangement. But, every spirit soars on Sunday morning when the masses simply sing! Friends, music, lessons, work, entertainment, inspiration, art!

### 7. THE TELETHON TALENT SHOW

There is so much organized talent in every community. There are rock bands and bluegrass bands, jazz, country and punk bands. There are men's choruses and women's choirs, jazz, pop, show, and traditional choruses. There are barbershoppers and tap dancers, baton twirlers, folk dancers, madrigal groups and square dancers. Think about it. The list goes on and on.

*Why not invite all of these groups to be a part of your all day musical showcase? Many communities now even have their own local cable television networks. If you have most of the television audience in your show there's a good chance that your cable folks would jump at a chance to televise it. Get a local celebrity to host it, or do it yourself, and go for it! You might even make it a telethon of sorts. Raise money for a good local cause that everyone agrees is important. Now...that's a trophy! Besides, it's plain fun to have everybody together for no other purpose than to share their music!*

### 8. SUMMER WORKSHOPS

*There really is no excuse now for not learning more about **The Art of Entertainment.** During the summer there are countless workshops and camps of varying lengths and concentrations dedicated precisely to this art. Some are directed toward young students, some toward teachers, and some toward both. Many are available for college credit. Most have some sort of culminating performance and almost all are worth your time. Nobody's going to take you by the hand and lead you to the workshop. You take the initiative! Once you're there, however, understanding professionals will take you by the hand and lead you through a non-threatening course that will make you a better person and a better producer. Check your choral journals, newsletters, etc. and read your "junk" mail for information on a workshop that best caters to your need. Go once! I promise you'll be hooked! See you there!*

*There are an unlimited number of variations to these examples of entertainment festivals. Tailor your Show to your audience, your performers, and yourself. Try to remember that **The Art of Entertainment** is a participatory art and a dynamic art. It changes constantly and grows incessantly. So, try not to get stuck in the Romantic period. Jump on the bandwagon. Keep one foot firmly planted in your fine, classical background and enjoy the arts of the historical masters. With the other foot try a little soft-shoe or do a full-blown tap dance! Some might suggest that there are people who are destined to live in this world as observers. But, as a "producer" of **The Art of Entertainment,** it is essential that you create your own, particular destiny as a "Participant!"*

> *"There are people who are destined to live in this world as observers. But, you create your own particular destiny as a 'Participant.'"*

### 9. AMERICA SINGS!

*"TO KIDS WHO FEEL THEY HAVE NO HOPE,
FROM KIDS WITH HOPE TO SHARE"*

*In the spring of 1987 I went jogging along the Potomoc River near my house in Washington D.C. There are hundreds of miles of paths reserved for bikers and runners, some of which take you directly under, around or even through our nation's treasured monuments. I stopped for a lemonade at George and Barbara's (The Watsons that is) and marveled at the wonderful backyard we call our nation's capitol.*

## 100% Positive

*I wheezed my way home and called Fritz with an idea that struck me as a fun way to spend a Saturday. "Let's get all of our musical friends (composers, arrangers, conductors, teachers, students, performers, publishers, etc.) together in the backyard and have a little celebration recognizing the role that music plays in all of our lives. We could set up a few stages, rent some sound equipment and really live it up! Maybe even at the end of the day we could all get together and have a big ol' singalong!"*

*And here's what makes Fritz Mountford exceptional...Without hesitation his response was, "You're nuts! Let's do it!"*

*On April 29, 1989 our little "singalong" became 450 schools, churches, community choirs and more, of all shapes, sizes, colors and creeds, totalling more than 15,000 singers. We filled 21 stages for a continuous string of performances and a huge mass event literally in the shadow of the Washington Monument! We even managed to raise a couple of hundred thousand dollars from the event that we gave away to organizations that help America's scores of homeless children.*

*In 1990 we took a bunch of America Singers and sang on both sides of the Berlin Wall as it came tumbling down!*

*In 1991 we brought our gathering out to four locations across the country. In Houston, Los Angeles, New York and Chicago another 13,000 singers demonstrated their "hope to share."*

*In a sentence (if that's possible...) America Sings is a non-profit, non-competitive choral festival that encourages it's participants of all ages to do what they love to do and at the same time help out less fortunate kids.*

*For more information please write or call:*

*America Sings, Inc.*
*6100A Old Franconia Road*
*Alexandria, VA 22310*
*703-922-8849*

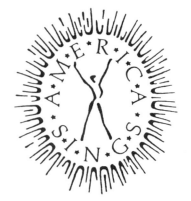

# COPYRIGHT LAW

It is, I think, a shame that the rules concerning copyright are often ignored. In searching for bigger, better, newer, and more unusual show segments, directors seem to feel free to dip into the reservoir of musical creations as though everything was in the Public Domain, thus, free to all. The rationalization is, "no one is *making money* from our borrowing." That seems to satisfy the conscience of a lot of people. But turn the rationalization around to "someone *is losing money* from our borrowing," and it just doesn't hold up.

Composers and publishers need to be compensated for their creations in order to insure the economic incentive for continued activity. They have to *pay* for the ink they write with, the paper they write on, the desk they write at. No one *gives* them a piano, or a studio, or a car, or lunch. If they can't trade what they make (songs) for what they need (groceries), eventually they'll go off and start making something else (anything but songs!). This is true even if you, the music teacher, use the composer's creations in the noble service of public education. The fact that you represent a school or church doesn't alter the fact that utility companies don't donate their water and lights to your school or church, the publishers don't donate their books, the custodians don't donate their time, and you don't donate your talent. Composers live in the same market-economy as the rest of the world.

I'm not a lawyer, so this isn't legal advice, but I want to share my understanding of the Copyright Law. The rights of a creator or owner of a copyright aren't uncertain. They are stated in the law and they are *exclusive* rights:

1. The Right to reproduce a copyrighted work.

2. The Right to perform publicly a copyrighted work.

3. The Right to prepare derivative works based on a copyrighted work.

4. The Right to distribute publicly a copyrighted work.

5. The Right to display publicly a copyrighted work.

The law is written, on purpose, to *exclude you* from copying, performing, fixing-up, distributing, and displaying someone else's property. That is very clear.

> *"Composers live in the same market economy as the rest of the world. They trade what they make for what they need."*

# Copyright Law

The law limits the rights of copyright holders in specific ways. It used to be that a concept called 'fair use' was vague, thus left certain uses of copyrighted works undefined. But the 1976 Copyright Law established precise limits of "fair use." You, as a teacher, are *allowed* to do certain, specific things:

1. You can make a copy of a lost part in an emergency if it is replaced with a purchased part "in due course."

2. You can make a *single* recording of a student performance for study and archive.

3. You can preserve or replace library copies if they're not available for purchase.

4. You can simplify or edit purchased copies provided the fundamental character of the work is not distorted.

On the other hand, you, as a teacher, are *forbidden* to do certain, specific things:

1. It is against the law to make copies to avoid purchase. (Show this to your administration or worship committee.)

2. It is against the law to make copies for any kind of performance. (Note the one, specific exception above.)

3. It is against the law to make a copy without including the copyright notice.

4. It is against the law to alter lyrics or to create lyrics if none exist.

There are, of course, a million other provisions, but the intent of the Copyright Law is clear. You must have permission to use someone else's copyrighted creation. The success of the Copyright Law depends on TRUST by composers and publishers, and on INTEGRITY by you and me!

*"The success of the copyright law depends on TRUST by composers and publishers, and on INTEGRITY by you and me!"*

# BIBLIOGRAPHY

## Suggested Reading

**The Contemporary Chorus**, Carl Strommen, 1980, Alfred, 126 pages, bibliography, discography.

 Major emphasis on vocal jazz sound and style. Definition, Harmony, Rhythm, Rhythm Section, Vocals and Band, Sound System, Rehearsal, Improvisation, Arranging/Publishers.

**Jazz and Show Choir Handbook**, Doug Anderson, 1978, Hinshaw, 150 pages, discography.

 The first comprehensive treatment of the subject. Organization/Rehearsal, Arrangements/Published Charts, Rhythm/Tone Color/Scat Singing, Accompaniment/Amplification/Packaging, Festivals, Publishers/Performance Rights.

**The Music Business**, Dick Weissman, 1979, Crown, 246 pages, index, glossary, bibliography.

 Deals with the nuts and bolts of making a living in the difficult world of professional entertainment and associated fields. Career Concerns, Recording, Agents, Publishing, Commercials, Unions, Engineering, Composing, Promotion, Education, Publishings, Criticism, Sales, Therapy, Repair, Arts Management. Contains a list of colleges offering programs in Music Business and an extensive annotated bibliography.

**Puttin' on the Glitz,** John Jacobson, 1983, Jenson, 68 pages, photographs.

 A basic vocabulary of movement based on simple marching. Includes a brief treatment of many peripheral topics. Basic Philosophy, Masculinity, Focus/Energy/Emotion.

**Vocal Jazz Concepts,** various authors, 1976, Hinshaw, 36 pages, bibliography, discography.

 Brief introduction to the basic elements of vocal jazz. Arranging, Rhythm Section, Ornamentation, Improvisation.

# Bibliography

**Vocal Jazz Style,** Kirby Shaw, 1987, Hal Leonard, second edition. Manual, Singer's Edition, Demonstration Cassette. Musical exercises and choral performance selections.

    Provides study exercises for 18 Vocal Jazz inflections and 3 full performance numbers.

**Warm-Ups For The Jazz And Show Choir,** Kirby Shaw, 1981, Hal Leonard. Package includes Score and 30 SATB parts.

    Basic vocal exercises for popular singing.

# Suggested Viewing

**Art Of Entertainment, The.** Fritz Mountford and John Jacobson, 1988, Hal Leonard. 60-minute VHS video tape companion to *The Art of Entertainment* Sourcebook.

Features teaching excerpts from *The Brightleaf Music Workshop, Ball State University Singers, Gotta Sing, Gotta Dance* and live choral performances.

**Gotta Sing, Gotta Dance,** John Jacobson, 1984, Hal Leonard. Four 60-minute VHS videotapes on the basics of choreography and staging.
Step 1 - The Basics Come First
Step 2 - Putting It All Together
Step 3 - Staging The Concert Performance
Step 4 - Movement and Staging For The Young Choir

Beginning to intermediate choreography instruction. John and student groups demonstrate all period dance styles. Includes live choral performances.

**If It Ain't Got Heart, It Ain't Art.**
John Jacobson, 1991, Hal Leonard. 25 minute VHS videotape.

**Publicity/Public Relations For The Choral Program.** Fritz Mountford, 1988, Hal Leonard. 45-minute VHS videotape.

Fritz teaches how to create a special identity for the school choral program. In class lecture at *Ball State University.*

**Vocal Production.** Fritz Mountford, 1988, Hal Leonard. 45-minute VHS videotape.

An "owner's manual" for singers. Fritz teaches the terms and mechanics of singing through practical exercises with the *Ball State University Singers.*

# Index

## A

Acknowledgements, xvi-xviii
A-position, 80
Abdominal muscles, 54
Abrupt ending, 118
Accented syllables, 71-72
Accompanist value, 10
Adam's apple, 55
Add-ons, 26
Administration, 39, 41, 112, 116, 123
Adult support group, 39
Advertising
    paid 35
    free, 33
    words and phrases, 37-38
Airport opening, 3-5
All American look, 107
All-Star cast, 139
Alphabet exercise, 53
America Sings!, 141-142
American English, 70-72, 74
American Sign language, 82
Amoeba, 90
Angels, 40
Anthems, Christmas, 22
Anticipation, program, 114-115
Applause, 118
    milking, 118
    peak, 118
    response, 118
Approach a mic, 84
Apron, costume 26
Apron, stage, 92
*Arabesque*, 92
Arlen, Harold 23
Arm garters, 26
Around the beat, 74
**Art of Entertainment Festivals,** 134-136
**Art of Entertainment Network,** 161
Articulation, 62-63
Aspiring young entertainers, 13
Attention to detail, 15, 105
**Audience,**
    analysis, 40
    core, 40
    diversity, 21
    point of view, 79, 123
Audience-oriented, 21

**Auditions,** 16-20
    deadline, 17
    package, 17
    dress, 18
    formal, 19
    live, 17-18
    taped, 16-17
Auditioner, 19-20
Avant Garde, 21-22

## B

Backstage, 13
Balance, staging, 77
Ballad, 24
Balm in Gilead, 69-70
Barbershop, 25
Barnum and Bailey, 90
Baroque Era, 24
Barrettes, 108
Beards, 107
Beat, play around, 74
Beethoven Society, 40
Bible School Songs, 24
Big Band Age, 23
Big Picture, 8
**Bibliography,** 145-147
**Biography,** 159
Black lights, 113
Black out, 91
Blimp, GOODYEAR™, 3
Blocks of color, 27
Bluegrass, 24
Boa, feathered, 26
Body mics, 85
Borge, Victor, 99
Bow, 81
    ensemble, 93-94
    individual, 82
    soloist, 81
Bow, hair, 26
Bowling pins, 80
Box Office, 13
Breed, Brian, xvii
Brightleaf Music Workshop, xvi
Broadway show tunes, 24
Brochure, 40
Budget, publicity, 33
Bustle, 26

# Index

## C

Calendar,
    publicity, 33
    rehearsal, 112
Call board, 110, 112
Captions, 35 (photo)
Carols, Christmas, 22
Cartoon characters, 95
Cassette, 16
Cast list, 20
Cattle call, 19
Caveman, 69
Cecil B. DeMille, xii
Chance, 16
Chant, 24
Charleston, 92
Cheerleaders, 31
Cheers, 91
Cherishing, 12
Chestnut, 99
Children, songs for, 25
Chinese Act, 119
Chivalry, 77
Choral festival, 138
Choralography, 77
**Choreography,** 89-97
    actor's approach, 89-90
    dancer's approach, 92-93
Christmas Carols,
    Anthems and Hymns, 22
Cinderellas, 19
Circus, 101
Clapping, 91, 118
Classical Period, 24
Clip-on tie, 26
Clothes as costumes, 27
Clump, 90
Combs, 108
Commercial Themes, 25
Common Job Description, 7
**Communication,** 65-76
Community service, 40
Community sing, 140
Company front, 91-92
Competition, 135

Conductor, 28
    costume, 28
    grooming, 107
Consonants, tuned 73-74
    stopped, 74-75
Consumers, 41
Contemporary Christian music, 22
Contents, v
Contest scoring, 132-134
Contrast, programming, 99
Controlled relaxation, 53
**Copyright law,** 143-144
Core audience, 40-41
Cosmetics, 108
Costume jewelry, 28
**Costumes,** 13, 26
    conductor, 28
    function, 32
    parade, 28
    value, 10
Costumes/Outfits, 13
Country cousins, 78
Country songs, 24
Cover letter, auditions, 17
Cowboy Folk Songs, 24
Creative people, 11
**Creativity,** 11-12
Crew, 112
Cross focus, 86
Cross-over, 96
Cup routine, 59
Curtain, 112
Curtain warmers, 110
Curtsy, 78

## D

Day One, 112
Dead air, 120
Dead pan, 78
Deadlines, 12
Debussy, Claude, 100
Depth of sound, 118
Diaphragm, 50-55
Dinner party, 123
Diphthongs, 72-73
Direction in choreography, 90
Director, choreography, 90

# Index

# Index

# Index

Two beat number, 101, 134
Two-choir position, 80
Type, personality, 16, 18

## U

**Ultimate Glitz,** 3-5
Unaccented syllables, 71-72
Uncle Sam, 100
Underdress, 32
Underlying pulse, 96
Unique identity, 43
Upstage, 83, 97
Ushers, 122
Uvula, 60

## V

V-position, 80
Value of accompanist's time, 10
    of costumes, 10
    of music, 9
    of entertainment, 9-10
    of performer's rehearsal time, 10
    of piano, 10
    of Producer/Director's time, 10
Varied publicity, 37
Vaudeville show, 124
Vibration, 55-56
Viewing, suggested, 147
Visual appeal, program, 116
Vital statistics, 117
Vocal cords, 55-56
Vocal warm-ups, 113
Vocal Jazz, 22
**Vocal Production,** Five T's of, 49-64
Volume, 71
Vowels, 72, 73

## W

Walt Disney World, xvi, 105
Waltz, 92
War eras, 25
Waring, Fred, iii, xv, 22, 23, 67
Warm ups, vocal, 113
Wedding reception, 54
Welcome, 123

Western songs, 24
White socks, 108-109
Wings, stage, 96
Wrinkles, 32
Written language, 63

## Z

Zero stance, 82
Zoot suit, 29

Now that you've read his book, I want to take a minute to brag about my friend, Fritz. If you've ever been a singer in one of his All-State festival choirs or attended one of his convention lectures, you know the excitement and enthusiasm he generates. Here is my favorite evaluation from a participant in the Brightleaf Music Workshop:

> "One hour with Fritz Mountford keeps me going for a year. He enlarges my capability, and reminds me of why I chose to be a teacher. He'll never know how many times I 're-play' his statements in my mind. Without a dose of the 'Fritz Philosophy' on an annual basis, I'd probably choose to start selling insurance — or else I'd simply retire!"

Thousands of teachers and his fellow clinicians, at camps and workshops and conventions around the country, would echo those sentiments. He has been a popular guest conductor, lecturer, and adjudicator in thirty-four states and in Europe. His Video Master Class lectures on Vocal Production and on Public Relations continue to be best sellers for Hal Leonard Publishing Corporation.

After you've seen him in action on the podium, it might surprise you to know that Fritz is a bona-fide college professor! He is the producer/director of the nationally renowned Ball State University Singers, who serve as Indiana's Official Goodwill Ambassadors. (Chances are you've seen them — they are the "class act" featured in a number of the Hal Leonard Showcase Videos!) At Ball State he also teaches a variety of graduate and undergraduate choral music classes, including an innovative seminar course for music educators based on his Art of Entertainment philosophy.

Fritz contributes to both the classical and the entertainment worlds. He was a vocal coach for the Walt Disney Company at Disneyland and at Walt Disney World, and toured America with Fred Waring's Pennsylvanians. In addition, he holds degrees from Hastings College in Nebraska and from the University of Miami in Florida. He has completed doctoral course work at the University of Missouri-Kansas City, and is writing the first scholarly study of pioneer choral conductor and showman Fred Waring.

Besides all this, Fritz has been involved with America Sings! longer than anybody else and serves behind the scenes as a member of the Board of Directors. A native of Red Cloud, Nebraska, he is a wonderful storyteller and a watercolor artist — in his spare time! All over the country, all year long, music educators conventions, All-State choirs, America Sings!, the Brightleaf Music Workshop, Fred Waring's U.S. Chorus, Show Choir Camps of America, Showstoppers National Invitational, and a gazillion other projects just wouldn't be the same without Fritz's magic touch. And I'm so glad that he's my friend!

# *The Art of Entertainment*
# Network

Now, *you're* a part of our system of energy. You have the exciting responsibility of *sharing the energy* by sharing your knowledge. If you would like to receive information on workshops, festivals and publications relating to **The Art of Entertainment**

**or**

share your experiences, ideas and thoughts regarding your choral performances, please write to:

**Fritz Mountford**
**The Art of Entertainment**
**Hal Leonard Publishing Corporation**
**P. O. Box 13819**
**Milwaukee, WI 53213**

| | |
|---|---|
| **Name** | |
| **School/Church** | |
| **Address** | |
| **City State Zip** | |
| **Home Address** | |
| **City State Zip** | |

You have our permission to photocopy this page from
**The Art of Entertainment.** Let us hear from you!